NORTHERN KNITS

NORTHERN KNITS

Designs inspired by
the knitting traditions of scandinavia,
iceland, and the shetland isles

LUCINDA GUY

INTERWEAVE.
interweavestore.com

Editor Ann Budd
Technical Editor Lori Gayle
Art Director Liz Quan
Cover and Interior Design Karla Baker
Layout Design Lee Calderon
Photographer Joe Hancock
Stylist Carol Beaver
Make-up & Hair Kathy MacKay
Illustrator Ann Swanson
Production Katherine Jackson

Interweave Press LLC
201 East Fourth Street
Loveland, CO 80537 USA
interweavestore.com

Printed in China by C&C Offset.

Library of Congress Cataloging-in-Publication Data
Guy, Lucinda.
 Northern knits : designs inspired by the knitting traditions of Scandinavia,
Iceland, and the Shetland Isles / Lucinda Guy.
    p. cm.
 Includes index.
 ISBN 978-1-59668-171-2 (pbk.)
 1. Knitting--Scandinavia. 2. Knitting--Iceland. 3. Knitting--Scotland--
Shetland. I. Title.
 TT819.S26G89 2010
 746.43'2--dc22

                    2009039517

10 9 8 7 6 5 4 3 2 1

Additional photography Page 4: (Swedish Cabin in the Snow) © Rhoberazzi, (Shetland Knitting) © Shetland Museum and Archives. Page 5: (Red Lichen) © Mattias Hagström. Page 8: (Silver Birch Trees) © Mikael Hjerpe, (Icelandic Window) © Brytta, (Shetland Knitting) © Shetland Museum and Archives, (Norwegian Landscape) © Tyler Olson, (Shetland Woman Knitting Fair Isle) © Shetland Museum and Archives, (Wooden Norwegian Figure and Knitted Reindeer) © François Hall. Page 9: (Balls of Icelandic Lace weight yarn and Carved Norwegian Doorway) © François Hall. Page 10: (Icelandic landscape) © Gloom. Page 11: (Icelandic Sweater) © François Hall and (Icelandic Sheep) © Ziutograf. Page 44: (Shetland landscape) © Paula Gent. Page 45: (Girl wearing a Shetland Cardigan) © Shetland Museum and Archives, (Balls of Shetland Yarn) © François Hall. Page 76: (Norwegian Fjords landscape) © Marek Slusarczyk. Page 77: (Norwegian Cardigan and balls of Norwegian yarn) © François Hall. Page 110: (Swedish Cabin in the Snow) © Rhoberazzi. Page 111: (Twined Mittens and Skeins of Swedish yarn) © François Hall.

ACKNOWLEDGMENTS

In memory of my father.

I am deeply grateful to all at Interweave for making this book
possible, and I extend heartfelt thanks to Eva and Francois for all their
help, support, patience, and understanding.

I also owe a considerable debt of gratitude to Connie at Jamieson & Smith,
Rebekka at Ístex, Siv at Dale of Norway, and Ann at Ullcentrum for supplying
me with their lovely yarns.

Thanks also to Shetland Museum, Francois Hall, Shutterstock, and iStock-
photo for permission to reproduce photographs.

CONTENTS

8   **Introduction**

10   **Iceland**
12   Hulda Striped Pullover
20   Ennid Laceweight Shawl
24   Unnur Icelandic Pullover
30   Yrsa Laceweight Mitts
36   Lilja Textured Jacket

44   **Shetland**
46   Crowning Glory Cobweb Shawl
52   Moth Short-Sleeved Top
58   Effie Fair Isle Pullover
66   Nell Shetland Cap
70   Hester Chevron Lace Pullover

76   **Norway**
78   Annemor Pullover
86   Thora Cardigan
96   Inger Ski Cap and Gloves
104   Liv Patterned Socks

110   **Sweden**
112   Ola Placket Pullover
122   Pia Laceweight Pullover
130   Märta Embroidered Bag
134   Ulla Twined Socks
140   Ottilia Twined Mittens

146   **Glossary**
158   **Sources for Supplies**
159   **Index**

NORTHERN knits

INTRODUCTION

The rich diversity and proliferation of folk art and handicrafts from the northern areas of Europe are owed in no small part to the long, dark, cold winters that forced people inside their homes during the endless winter months. The home and everything relating to it was all-important, and it was only natural that attention and care was taken to transform everyday domestic objects into handsome decorative pieces, and that many hours were spent knitting and stitching impressive, beautiful clothes for festive occasions. Folk handicrafts are directly representative of the people who made them, the way in which they lived, their customs, how they survived and managed their lives.

I have always been deeply interested in northern European folk art, and since I first started designing, I have been heavily influenced by traditional folk textiles. Shetland, Iceland, Norway, and Sweden have always held a particular fascination for me, each with a rich heritage of unique knitted folk art—Fair Isle sweaters, Shetland lace shawls, Icelandic Lopi sweaters, Norwegian black-and-white Selbu mittens, and Swedish twined knitted mittens.

Our lives are still influenced by the cycles of the natural world, by the rhythms of the seasons, and, despite our central heating and cheap, mass-made woolens, handknitting remains an expression for beautiful, protective, and warm clothing. The designs in this book, all of which are knitted in purl woolen yarns unique to each country, are knitted in true handicraft fashion—they are not only inspired directly from the past but include elements from a rich heritage of folk art to create something new and contemporary.

ICELAND

Iceland is an island of volcanoes, glaciers, waterfalls, faraway fells, and sunsets, and until modern times, was a remote, harsh, and often intense place to live. The first Viking settlers arrived in Iceland in the ninth century, bringing with them horses and sheep and establishing a vigorous trade in wool and woolen goods. Knitting was introduced to Iceland via England or northern Europe, and by the mid 1500s, was widespread and used to make clothes for both domestic use and trade. Because wool was abundant and knitting needles quick and cheap to make, knitting was accessible to even the poorest, most isolated farmers. Fleece was prepared by men and spun by women, and everyone knitted—even children as young as four years old. During the long, cold, dark winters, families gathered around the fire to work and knit as they listened to full-blooded sagas of Icelandic battles.

Although essentially a commercial activity, spinning and knitting became an integral part of Icelandic life. Wool was used as currency and long distances were measured by the number of knitted shoe linings worn out with walking. Folklore has it that witches would steal wool from farmers with the help of a "carrier" made by wrapping the rib bone of a recently buried man in gray wool to appear like a real hank of wool and then nurturing it until it gained life. Once brought to life, the fast-traveling carrier would zoom across the countryside, stealing fleece for the witch.

The majority of early Icelandic knitted garments, such as jackets, mittens, and long stockings, were plain and simply knitted out of naturally occurring colors of fleece. Pattern knitting developed in the 1600s, as evidenced by pattern books of embroidery and weaving designs found in Iceland dating from around this time. Later, beautiful naturalistic patterns of plants, leaves, and undulating lines similar to those found inside these books, were used to decorate clothes for special and festive occasions.

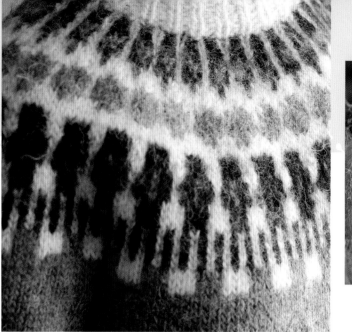

As was common throughout northern Europe, industrialization in the late 1800s brought about a decline in rural folk handicrafts. An influx of accessible new designs made it fashionable to knit with very delicate woolen yarn on incredibly fine needles to make openwork lace shawls, mittens, and wrist warmers. As spinning mills began to take over from the more traditional domestic methods of spinning, new ideas and methods of knitting started to emerge.

In the 1920s, a local Icelandic woman successfully experimented with knitting prespun, thick strands of industrially prepared fleece known as Lopi, and by the 1930s and 1940s, it was fashionable to use Lopi to knit lice-stitch patterned sweaters similar to traditional Norwegian sweaters. In the 1950s, a new style of sweater emerged from Sweden and Norway, incorporating elaborately patterned yokes or bands of patterns resembling a collar. In 1957, influenced by these trends, the first designs for the now traditional Icelandic Lopi sweater appeared.

The dramatically contrasting, unique colors of the Icelandic landscape and the outstanding quality of Icelandic wool—light and superbly insulating—inspired the projects in this section. My first trip to Iceland left me with vivid memories of strewn driftwood, black and gray volcanic beaches edged with bleached grasses, and dramatic bright orange lichens and fungi. These projects use classic Alafoss Lopi, Létt-Lopi, and Loðband laceweight yarns, all of which are manufactured exclusively by Ístex of Iceland from pure Icelandic wool supplied by Icelandic farmers. The projects, traditionally knitted in the round, are a celebration of the age-old use of wool to protect and cosset. Each garment is just as easily worn indoors or out, alone or wrapped and layered.

Hulda Striped
PULLOVER

FINISHED SIZE

32½ (36¾, 41, 45, 50)" (82.5 [93.5, 104, 114.5, 127] cm) bust circumference. Sweater shown measures 36¾" (93.5 cm).

YARN

Laceweight (#0 Lace).
Shown here: Loðband Einband (100% Icelandic wool; 246 yd [225 m]/50 g): #0059 black (MC), 4 (4, 5, 6, 6) balls; #1026 gray/white (D), 2 (2, 3, 3, 3) balls; #9939 beetroot (dark red; A), #9009 crimson (B), #0047 scarlet (C), #1027 light gray (E), #9102 medium gray (F), #9103 dark gray (G), #0151 gray/black (H), 1 ball each.

NEEDLES

Size 3 mm (no exact U.S. equivalent; between U.S. sizes 2 and 3): 16" and 32" (40 and 60 cm) circular (cir), and set of 4 or 5 double-pointed (dpn). Adjust needle size if necessary to obtain the correct gauge.

NOTIONS

Markers (m); stitch holder; removable markers; tapestry needle.

GAUGE

32 stitches and 38 rounds = 4" (10 cm) in stockinette stitch, worked in rounds.

Ístex Loðband laceweight yarn is available in a magnificently dramatic palette, ranging from deep sea blues and greens to glacial white and lava reds, from volcanic blacks to soft natural browns and grays, all obviously inspired by the often intense and violent natural colors found in the Icelandic landscape.

An easy-to-wear, gently fitted, yoked sweater, Hulda is every bit Icelandic—knitted in the finest, purest Icelandic wool in dark and brooding gradating tones. The darkest blacks blend to the lightest grays with volcanic tones of red as highlights.

BODY

With MC and longer cir needle, CO 292 (326, 360, 392, 432) sts. Place marker (pm) and join for working in rnds, being careful not to twist sts; rnd begins at left side "seam" at start of front sts. Work in k1, p1 rib for 6 rnds—piece measures about ¾" (2 cm). Change to St st and knit 1 rnd, pm after the first 146 (163, 180, 196, 216) sts to mark right side "seam"—146 (163, 180, 196, 216) sts each for front and back.

Rnd 1: *K1 with MC, k1 with A; rep from *.

Rnds 2 and 3: Knit with A.

Rnd 4: *K1 with A, k1 with B; rep from *.

Rnd 5: Knit with B.

Rnd 6: *K1 with B, k1 with C; rep from *.

Rnd 7: Knit with C.

Rnd 8: *K1 with C, k1 with D; rep from *.

Rnds 9–11: Knit with D.

Rnd 12: (dec rnd) With D, *k1, k2tog, knit to 2 sts before m, ssk, slip marker (sl m); rep from * once more—4 sts dec'd.

Rnds 13–20: Knit with D.

Rnd 21: *K1 with D, k1 with E; rep from *.

Rnd 22: Knit with E.

Rnd 23: *K1 with E, k1 with F; rep from *.

Rnd 24: With F, rep Rnd 12—4 sts dec'd.

Rnd 25: *K1 with F, k1 with G; rep from *.

Rnd 26: Knit with G.

Rnd 27: *K1 with G, k1 with H; rep from *.

Rnd 28: Knit with H.

Rnd 29: *K1 with H, k1 with MC; rep from *.

Rnd 30: Knit with MC.

Rnd 31: *K1 with MC, k1 with H; rep from *.

Rnd 32: Knit with H.

Rnd 33: *K1 with H, k1 with G; rep from *.

Rnd 34: Knit with G.

Rnd 35: *K1 with G, k1 with F; rep from *.

Rnd 36: With F, rep Rnd 12—4 sts dec'd.

Rnd 37: *K1 with F, k1 with E; rep from *.

Rnd 38: Knit with E.

Rnd 39: *K1 with E, k1 with D; rep from *.

Rnds 40–47: Knit with D.

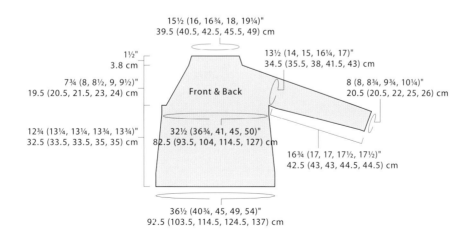

15½ (16, 16¾, 18, 19¼)"
39.5 (40.5, 42.5, 45.5, 49) cm

1½"
3.8 cm

13½ (14, 15, 16¼, 17)"
34.5 (35.5, 38, 41.5, 43) cm

7¾ (8, 8½, 9, 9½)"
19.5 (20.5, 21.5, 23, 24) cm

8 (8, 8¾, 9¾, 10¼)"
20.5 (20.5, 22, 25, 26) cm

Front & Back

12¾ (13¼, 13¼, 13¾, 13¾)"
32.5 (33.5, 33.5, 35, 35) cm

32½ (36¾, 41, 45, 50)"
82.5 (93.5, 104, 114.5, 127) cm

16¾ (17, 17, 17½, 17½)"
42.5 (43, 43, 44.5, 44.5) cm

36½ (40¾, 45, 49, 54)"
92.5 (103.5, 114.5, 124.5, 137) cm

Rnd 48: With D, rep Rnd 12—4 sts dec'd; 276 (310, 344, 376, 416) sts rem.

Cont stripe patt as foll and *at the same time* work a dec rnd on Rnds 60, 72, 84, and 96:

Rnds 49—67: Rep Rnds 21—39—4 sts dec'd.

Rnds 68—72: Knit with D—4 sts dec'd.

Rnds 73—91: Rep Rnds 21—39—4 sts dec'd.

Rnds 92—94: Knit with D.

Rnds 95—103: Rep Rnds 21—29, ending with a rnd of H and MC—260 (294, 328, 360, 400) sts rem.

Knit 11 (15, 15, 19, 19) rnds with MC—piece measures 12¾ (13¼, 13¼, 13¾, 13¾)" (32.5 [33.5, 33.5, 35, 35] cm) from CO.

Next rnd: With MC, BO 6 (7, 8, 8, 9) sts, knit to 6 (7, 8, 8, 9) sts before side m, BO 12 (14, 16, 16, 18) sts removing side m in center of BO, knit to last 6 (7, 8, 8, 9) sts, BO rem sts—118 (133, 148, 164, 182) sts each for front and back.

Leaving sts on needle, break yarn, and set aside.

Sleeves

With MC and dpn, CO 64 (64, 70, 78, 82) sts. Pm and join for working in rnds, being careful not to twist sts. Work k1, p1 rib for 6 rnds—piece measures about ¾" (2 cm). Change to St st.

Rnds 1—8: Work stripe patt as for body.

Rnd 9: Knit with D,

Rnd 10: (inc rnd) With D, k2, M1 (see Glossary), knit to last 2 sts, M1, k2—2 sts inc'd.

Rnds 11—26: Knit with D, inc 2 sts every 6th rnd (on Rnds 16 and 22)—70 (70, 76, 84, 88) sts.

Rnds 27–45: Work stripe patt as for Rnds 21–39 of body, omitting body decs, and instead inc 2 sts every 6th rnd (on sleeve Rnds 28, 34, and 40)—76 (76, 82, 90, 94) sts.

Rnds 46–140: Work stripe patt as for Rnds 9–103 of body, omitting body decs and instead inc 2 sts every 6th rnd (on sleeve Rnds 46, 52, 58, 64, 70, 76, 82, 88, 94, 100, 106, 112, 118, 124, 130, and 136), changing to shorter cir needle when there are too many sts to fit on dpn—108 (108, 114, 122, 126) sts.

Knit 11 (15, 15, 19, 19) rnds with MC and *at the same time* inc 2 sts every 0 (6, 4, 4, 3) rnds 0 (2, 3, 4, 5) times—108 (112, 120, 130, 136) sts; piece measures 16¾ (17, 17, 17½, 17½)" (42.5 [43, 43, 44.5, 44.5] cm) from CO.

Next rnd: With MC, BO 6 (7, 8, 8, 9) sts, knit to last 6 (7, 8, 8, 9) sts, BO rem sts—96 (98, 104, 114, 118) sts. Break yarn and place sts on holder.

Make second sleeve the same as the first, place sts on shorter cir needle if they are not already on the cir needle. Do not break yarn.

Yoke

Joining rnd: With MC and longer cir needle holding body sts, k96 (98, 104, 114, 118) left sleeve sts from shorter cir needle, k118 (133, 148, 164, 182) front sts, place held right sleeve sts on shorter cir needle, k96 (98, 104, 114, 118) right sleeve sts, k118 (133, 148, 164, 182) back sts—428 (462, 504, 556, 600) sts total.

Place m and join for working in rnds; rnd begins at left back at start of left sleeve sts. Work in St st with MC as foll:

Next rnd: Knit, inc 1 (0, 2, 5, 5) st(s) evenly spaced—429 (462, 506, 561, 605) sts.

Knit 18 (18, 23, 23, 28) rnds.

Dec Rnd 1: *K9, k2tog; rep from *—390 (420, 460, 510, 550) sts rem.

Knit 7 (8, 8, 9, 9) rnds.

Dec Rnd 2: *K4, k2tog, k4; rep from *—351 (378, 414, 459, 495) sts rem.

Knit 6 (7, 7, 8, 8) rnds.

Dec Rnd 3: *K12 (12, 16, 11, 13), k2tog; rep from * to last 1 (0, 0, 4, 0) st(s), k1 (0, 0, 4, 0)—326 (351, 391, 424, 462) sts rem.

Knit 5 (6, 6, 7, 7) rnds.

Dec Rnd 4: *K5, k2tog, k6; rep from * to last 1 (0, 1, 8, 7) st(s), k2tog 0 (0, 0, 1, 1) time, k1 (0, 1, 6, 5)—301 (324, 361, 391, 426) sts rem.

Knit 5 (5, 5, 6, 6) rnds.

Dec Rnd 5: Work according to your size as foll:
Size 32½": *[K9, k2tog] 2 times, [k10, k2tog] 3 times; rep from * to last 11 sts, k9, k2tog—275 sts.
Size 36¾": *K10, k2tog; rep from *—297 sts.
Size 41": *K9, k2tog, [k10, k2tog] 2 times; rep from * to last 11 sts, k9, k2tog—330 sts.
Size 45": K9, k2tog, *k8, k2tog; rep from *—352 sts.
Size 50": *[K6, k2tog] 4 times, k7, k2tog; rep from * to last 16 sts, [k6, k2tog] 2 times—374 sts.

Knit 5 rnds.

Dec Rnd 6: *K5, k2tog, k4; rep from *—250 (270, 300, 320, 340) sts rem.

Knit 4 rnds.

Dec Rnd 7: *K8, k2tog; rep from *—225 (243, 270, 288, 306) sts rem.

Knit 4 rnds.

Dec Rnd 8: *K4, k2tog, k3; rep from *—200 (216, 240, 256, 272) sts rem.

Knit 3 rnds.

Dec Rnd 9: *K6, k2tog; rep from *—175 (189, 210, 224, 238) sts rem.

Knit 2 rnds.

Dec Rnd 10: *K3, k2tog, k2; rep from *—150 (162, 180, 192, 204) sts rem.

Knit 1 rnd.

Dec Rnd 11: *K2tog, k13 (7, 4, 4, 4); rep from *—140 (144, 150, 160, 170) sts rem; yoke measures about 7¾ (8, 8½, 9, 9½)" (19.5 [20.5, 21.5, 23, 24] cm) from joining rnd.

NECKBAND

Rnd 1: K15 (16, 16, 16, 16), k1 and hang a removable m in this st, k69 (71, 74, 79, 84), k1 and hang a removable m in this st, k54 (55, 58, 63, 68)—marked sts are at each side of neck; move the markers up as you work so you can always identify the marked sts.

Rnd 2: (dec rnd) *Knit to 2 sts before marked st, ssk, k1 (marked st), k2tog; rep from * once more, knit to end—4 sts dec'd.

Rnds 3–14: Knit, dec 4 sts as for Rnd 2 on Rnds 5, 8, and 11, then dec 0 (0, 2, 0, 2) sts evenly spaced in Rnd 14—124 (128, 132, 144, 152) sts rem; neckband measures about 1½" (3.8 cm); Rnd 14 is neckband fold line.

Rnd 15: *Knit to 1 st before marked st, M1, k1, k1 (marked st), k1, M1; rep from * once more, knit to end—128 (132, 136, 148, 156) sts.

Rnds 16–17: *K3, p1; rep from *.

Rnd 18: (inc rnd) *Work in established rib to 1 st before marked st, M1, k1, k1 (marked st), k1, M1; rep from * once more, work in rib to end—132 (136, 140, 152, 160) sts.

FINISHING

Rnds 19–26: Cont in established rib, inc 4 sts as for Rnd 18 on Rnds 21 and 24, working new sts into rib patt—140 (144, 148, 160, 168) sts.
Rnd 27: Knit.
BO all sts loosely.

Weave in loose ends. With MC threaded on a tapestry needle, sew small underarm seams. Fold neckband in half to WS and slip-stitch invisibly in place with MC threaded on a tapestry needle.

Carefully handwash, roll in a towel to remove moisture, then block to correct size and allow to dry completely.

ENNID LACEWEIGHT
SHAWL

FINISHED SIZE

About 82" (208.5 cm) wide across top edge and 23½" (59.5 cm) long from center of top edge to tip of lower point.

YARN

Laceweight (#0 Lace).
Shown here: Loðband Einband (100% Icelandic wool; 246 yd [225 m]/50 g): #9720 green, 5 balls.

NEEDLES

Size U.S. 3 (3.25 mm): 32" or 40" (80 or 100 cm) circular (cir). Adjust needle size if necessary to obtain the correct gauge.

NOTIONS

Tapestry needle.

GAUGE

26 stitches and 44 rows = 4" (10 cm) in garter stitch.

Simple, lace-light, and practical, the Ennid Shawl is reminiscent of the traditional garter-stitch triangular shawls once worn by Icelandic women on a daily basis. Traditionally, this type of shawl was worn wrapped across the chest and tied at the back, a look that is still nice today. Or, wrap the Ennid Shawl around your neck and shoulders and knot or pin it in place. Either way, it provides a superb insulating layer. The small knitted edging lends an extra textural detail, which, once the shawl has been hand washed, softens and shapes up nicely.

NOTES

· The shawl is worked from side to side as a
wide, shallow triangle. It begins at one top
point, increases gradually along one selvedge
to the center, then decreases to the other
top point. The unshaped selvedge forms the
straight top edge.

· For a larger or smaller shawl, repeat Rows 7–12
more or fewer times for the first half of the
shawl, then repeat Rows 1–6 for the second
half until 2 stitches remain. Every 12 rows
(2 repeats) added or removed on each side
of center will increase or decrease the overall
width by about 2¼" (5.5 cm) and the length
from the top edge to lower point by about
¾" (2 cm).

Shawl

CO 2 sts. Inc for first half of shawl as foll:

Rows 1 (RS) and 2 (WS): Knit.

Row 3: K1f&b, k1—3 sts.

Rows 4 and 5: Knit.

Row 6: K1, k1f&b, k1—4 sts.

Rows 7 and 8: Knit.

Row 9: K1f&b, knit to end—1 st inc'd.

Rows 10 and 11: Knit.

Row 12: Knit to last 2 sts, k1f&b, k1—1 st inc'd.

Rep Rows 7–12 for patt 73 more times, or as desired (see Notes)—152 sts. Knit 2 rows—piece measures about 41" (104 cm) from CO.

Dec for second half of shawl as foll:

Row 1: K1, k2tog, knit to end—1 st dec'd.

Rows 2 and 3: Knit.

Row 4: Knit to last 3 sts, k2tog, k1—1 st dec'd.

Rows 5 and 6: Knit.

Rep Rows 1–6 for patt 74 more times—2 sts rem. Knit 2 rows—piece measures about 82" (208.5 cm) from CO. BO all sts.

EDGING

Hold shawl with RS facing and straight top edge running across the bottom of the "pyramid" and join yarn to corner at right-hand side. With cir needle, pick up and knit 339 sts along shaped selvedge to center point (3 sts for every 4 rows), then 339 sts along other shaped edge to corner at left-hand side—678 sts total.

Row 1: (WS) *Insert tip of right needle into st on left needle as if to knit, wrap the yarn completely around tip of both needles once, then wrap the yarn around the right needle as if to knit and draw through a loop, then slip the old st and the wrap from the left needle; rep from * to end.

Note: This method of making elongated stitches is slightly different from wrapping the yarn twice around the needle for each stitch. This elongated stitch is formed in a single step, without having to drop any extra wraps on the following row, and will appear twisted at its base.

Row 2: (RS) Working all sts in the usual manner, BO 1 st, *work [k1, p1] 2 times in next st, turn work, BO 4 sts, turn work, slip first st on left needle to right needle, BO 2 sts; rep from * to end, fasten off last st.

Finishing

Weave in loose ends. Carefully handwash shawl according to yarn label instructions, roll in a towel to remove moisture, block to correct size, and allow to dry.

Unnur Icelandic
PULLOVER

FINISHED SIZE

About 34 1/4 (41, 48, 54 3/4)" (87 [104, 122, 139] cm) bust/chest circumference.
Sweater shown measures 41" (104 cm).

YARN

Chunky weight (#5 Bulky).
Shown here: Alafoss Lopi (100% wool; 109 yd [100 m]/100 g): #0053 brown (MC), 7 (8, 9, 10) balls; #0051 off-white (A), 2 (2, 3, 3) balls; #9973 tan heather (B) and #0867 dark brown (C), 1 ball each.

NEEDLES

Size U.S. 10 (6 mm): 12", 24", and 40" (30, 60, and 100 cm) circular (cir). Adjust needle size if necessary to obtain the correct gauge.

NOTIONS

Marker (m); stitch holders; tapestry needle.

GAUGE

14 stitches and 18 rounds = 4" (10 cm) in solid-color stockinette stitch, worked in rounds; 14 stitches and 17 rounds = 4" (10 cm) in stockinette colorwork pattern from charts, worked in rounds.

Knitted in light and insulating Alafoss Lopi, this pullover is uniquely suited to wearing outdoors—it is naturally 100 percent guaranteed to keep you warm and cozy!

On my first trip to Iceland more than twenty years ago, I discovered the delights of Icelandic wool, and I bought myself the loveliest of Lopi cardigans, which I still have and wear to this day—it is one of my most treasured items. If you knit a Lopi sweater, you will knit a sweater for life!

SLEEVES

With MC and shortest cir needle, CO 42 sts for all sizes. Place marker (pm) and join for working in rnds, being careful not to twist sts. Work in k1, p1 rib for 6 rnds—piece measures about 1½" (3.8 cm) from CO. Knit 1 rnd, inc 6 sts evenly spaced—48 sts. Knit 2 rnds. Work Rnds 1–9 of Star chart (see page 28) in stranded St st, beg and ending where indicated for sleeve and *at the same time* inc 1 st each side of m on Rnd 5, working new sts in MC—50 sts. When chart has been completed, cont in St st with MC and knit 3 rnds, then *inc 1 st each side of m on next rnd, knit 12 (4, 4, 2) rnds, inc 1 st each side of m on next rnd, knit 15 (7, 7, 5) rnds; rep from * 0 (1, 2, 3) more time(s), changing to medium-length cir needle if necessary for your size—54 (58, 62, 66) sts. Cont even with MC until piece measures 17 (18, 18¼, 18½)" (43 [45.5, 46.5, 47] cm) from CO,

ending 4 (5, 5, 5) sts before end-of-rnd marker. Break yarn, leaving a 30" (76 cm) tail for grafting later. Place last 4 (5, 5, 5) sts of rnd and first 3 (4, 4, 4) sts of next rnd on holder for underarm— 7 (9, 9, 9) sts on holder. Place rem 47 (49, 53, 57) sleeve sts on separate holder or waste yarn. Make second sleeve in the same manner.

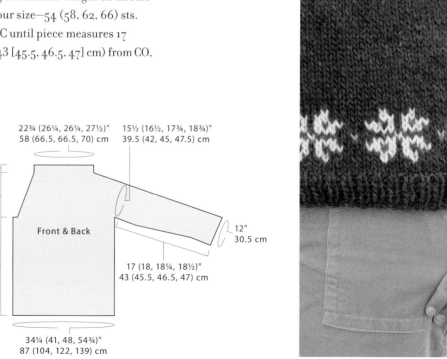

22¾ (26¼, 26¼, 27½)"
58 (66.5, 66.5, 70) cm

15½ (16½, 17¾, 18¾)"
39.5 (42, 45, 47.5) cm

1¼"
3.2 cm

8 (8, 9, 9¾)"
20.5 (20.5, 23, 25) cm

Front & Back

16 (16, 17, 17)"
40.5 (40.5, 43, 43) cm

12"
30.5 cm

17 (18, 18¼, 18½)"
43 (45.5, 46.5, 47) cm

34¼ (41, 48, 54¾)"
87 (104, 122, 139) cm

LOWER BODY

With MC and medium-length or longest cir needle (as needed for your size), CO 120 (144, 168, 192) sts. Pm and join for working in rnds, being careful not to twist sts. Work in k1, p1 rib for 6 rnds—piece measures about 1½" (3.8 cm) from CO. Change to St st and knit 3 rnds. Work Rnds 1–9 of Star chart in stranded St st, beg and end as indicated for body. Work even in St st with MC until piece measures 16 (16, 17, 17)" (40.5 [40.5, 43, 43] cm) from CO, ending 4 (5, 5, 5) sts before end-of-rnd marker.

DIVIDE FOR FRONT AND BACK

Knit the last 4 (5, 5, 5) sts of rnd and first 3 (4, 4, 4) sts of next rnd and place 7 (9, 9, 9) sts just worked on holder for underarm, k53 (63, 75, 87), k7 (9, 9, 9) and place 7 (9, 9, 9) sts just worked on another holder for other underarm, k53 (63, 75, 87) to end. Do not break yarn. Transfer body sts to longest cir needle if they are not already on it.

	brown		dark brown
•	off-white	☐	pattern repeat
×	tan heather		

STAR

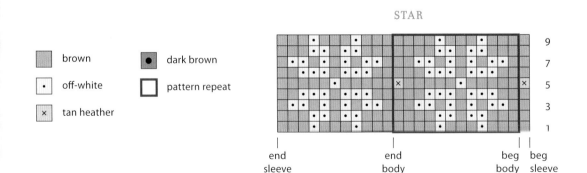

YOKE

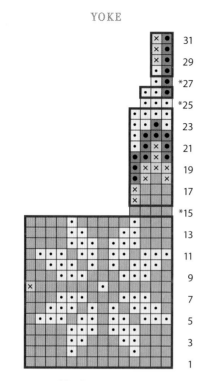

*See instructions.

rnds on yoke chart are indicated by *; work the dec rnds as indicated in the instructions, changing to progressively shorter cir as necessary.

Dec Rnd 1: (Rnd 15 of chart) With MC, k3 (3, 7, 2), [k2tog, k3, k2tog, k4] 16 (19, 21, 24) times, [k2tog, k3 (4, 5, 2)] 3 (2, 2, 3) times, k2tog 1 (0, 0, 1) time—160 (184, 208, 228) sts rem.

Work Rnds 16–24 of chart.

Dec Rnd 2: (Rnd 25 of chart) With A, *k2tog, k2; rep from *—120 (138, 156, 171) sts rem.

Work Rnd 26 of chart.

Dec Rnd 3: (Rnd 27 of chart) *K1 with C, k2tog with A; rep from *—80 (92, 104, 114) sts rem.

Work Rnds 28–31 of chart. With MC, knit 1 rnd, dec 0 (0, 12, 18) sts evenly spaced—80 (92, 92, 96) sts rem; yoke measures about 8 (8, 9, 9¾)" (20.5 [20.5, 23, 25] cm) from joining rnd.

NECKBAND

With MC, work in k1, p1 rib for 2¾" (7 cm). Break yarn, leaving a tail about 3 times the length of the neck opening.

Yoke

Joining rnd: *With RS facing, place 47 (49, 53, 57) held sleeve sts on left needle, k47 (49, 53, 57) left sleeve sts, k53 (63, 75, 87) front sts; rep from * once more for right sleeve and back—200 (224, 256, 288) sts total; 53 (63, 75, 87) sts each for front and back; 47 (49, 53, 57) sts each sleeve; rnd beg at left back and starts with left sleeve sts.

With MC, knit 1 (1, 6, 9) rnd(s), dec 4 (0, 4, 8) sts evenly spaced in last rnd—196 (224, 252, 280) sts. Work Rnds 1–14 of Yoke chart. *Note:* Dec

Finishing

Fold neckband in half to WS and, with yarn threaded on a tapestry needle, whipstitch (see Glossary) live sts to the base of the neckband, taking care to match the elasticity of the knitted fabric so the neck opening will not be too tight. With tails threaded on a tapestry needle, graft live sts at underarms using the Kitchener st (see Glossary). Weave in loose ends.

Steam-block lightly using a warm iron over a damp cloth.

URSA LACEWEIGHT
MITTS

FINISHED SIZE

About 7½" (19 cm) hand circumference,
and 6" (15 cm) long.

YARN

Laceweight (#0 Lace).
Shown here: Loðband Einband (100% wool; 246
yd [225 m]/50 g): #9720 straw (A), #1026 ash (B),
#9934 orange (C), and #0437 storm blue (D),
1 ball each.

NEEDLES

Size 2.5 mm (no U.S. equivalent; between U.S. sizes
1 and 2): set of 5 double-pointed (dpn). Adjust
needle size if necessary to obtain the correct gauge.

NOTIONS

Marker (m); stitch holder; tapestry needle.

GAUGE

16 stitches and 18 rounds = 2" (5 cm) in stranded
stockinette colorwork from charts, worked in
rounds, before blocking.

Laceweight yarn has traditionally been used by
Icelanders to knit patterned mittens and *hand-stukur* (long, lacy wrist warmers); these practical
little mitts fall neatly between these two types of
hand wear. With some simple calculations, the
pattern could easily be extended to make mittens
or simplified to make wrist warmers.

Knitted in Ístex's Loðband, these mitts must
be washed before wearing, allowing the yarn to
soften and felt slightly. The color palette available
for Loðband ranges from soft tonal shades to
strong, dramatic colors—all reflective of the varied
natural colors of Iceland.

HAND

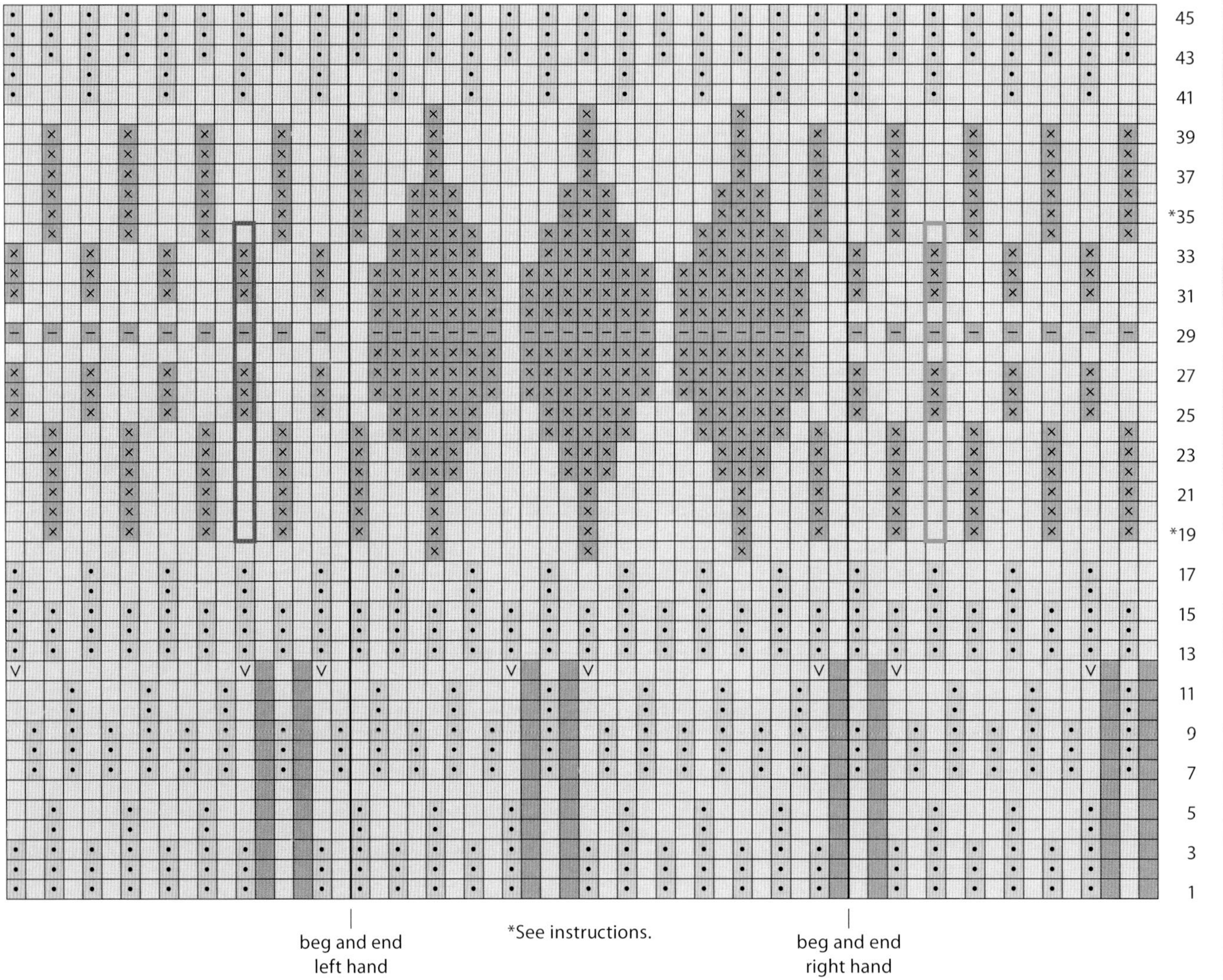

45
43
41
39
37
*35
33
31
29
27
25
23
21
*19
17
15
13
11
9
7
5
3
1

| beg and end left hand | *See instructions. | beg and end right hand |

straw
ash
orange

storm blue
k1f&b with ash
no stitch

right thumb placement
left thumb placement

RIGHT MITT

With A, CO 52 sts. Arrange sts evenly on 4 dpn (13 sts on each needle), place marker (pm), and join for working in rnds; rnd beg at little finger side of hand. Work in k1, p1 rib for 6 rnds—piece measures about ¾" (2 cm). Establish patt from Rnd 1 of Hand chart as foll: Beg where indicated for right hand, work the last 39 sts of chart, then work the first 13 sts of chart to end where indicated. Work Rnds 2–11 of chart, then work Rnd 12, inc 8 sts as shown—60 sts. Work even in patt through Rnd 18 of chart—piece measures about 2¾" (7 cm) from CO.

SHAPE GUSSET

Rnd 19: Work 31 sts in patt, pm, k1f&b in next st shown by thumb placement outline (k1f&b counts as Rnd 19 of Right Thumb chart), pm, work 28 sts to end—61 sts; 2 sts between thumb m. Substituting Right Thumb chart for sts at outlined position, work through Rnd 34 of both charts, working k1f&b in first st of thumb section in Rnds 20–28 as shown on thumb chart—70 sts; 11 thumb sts between markers.

Rnd 35: Work in patt to marked thumb sts, then removing thumb markers as you come to them, place the next 18 sts on holder for thumb, use the backward-loop method (see Glossary) to CO 8 sts over gap in colors to maintain chart patt, work in patt to end—60 sts rem.

UPPER HAND

Work through Rnd 45 of Hand chart. With A, work in k1, p1 rib for 2 rnds—piece measures about 6" (15 cm) from CO. BO all sts as foll to draw in the upper edge: *BO 4 sts, k2tog (2 sts on right needle), pass 1 st on right needle over dec st to BO 1 st; rep from * to end.

THUMB

Place 18 held thumb sts on dpn and rejoin yarns to beg of thumb sts with RS facing. Work 18 sts patt from Rnd 35 of Right Thumb chart, then pick up and knit 8 sts from base of sts CO over thumb gap in colors to cont chart patt—26 sts total. Arrange sts so that there are 6 sts on Needle 1, 7 sts on Needle 2, 6 sts on Needle 3, and 7 sts on Needle 4. Work in patt through Rnd 41 of chart. With A, work in k1, p1 rib for 2 rnds—thumb measures about 1" (2.5 cm) from pick-up rnd. BO all sts as for upper hand to draw in upper edge of thumb.

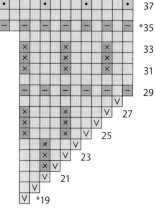

RIGHT THUMB

*See instructions.

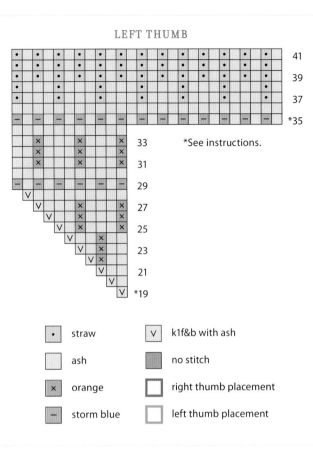

LEFT THUMB

																				41
																				39
																				37
																				*35

33
31
29
27
25
23
21
*19

*See instructions.

	straw			k1f&b with ash
	ash			no stitch
	orange			right thumb placement
	storm blue			left thumb placement

LEFT MITT

With A, CO 52 sts. Arrange sts on needles and work 6 rnds in k1, p1 rib as for right mitt—piece measures about ¾" (2 cm). Establish patt from Rnd 1 of Hand chart as foll: Beg where indicated for left hand, work the last 16 sts of chart, then work the first 36 sts of chart to end where indicated. Work Rnds 2–11 of chart, then work Rnd 12 inc 8 sts as shown—60 sts. Work even through Rnd 18 of chart—piece measures about 2¾" (7 cm) from CO.

SHAPE GUSSET

Rnd 19: Work 29 sts in patt, pm, k1f&b in next st shown by thumb placement outline (k1f&b counts as Rnd 19 of Left Thumb chart), pm, work 30 sts to end—61 sts; 2 sts between thumb m. Substituting Left Thumb chart for sts at outlined position, work through Rnd 34 of both charts, working k1f&b in last st of thumb section in Rnds 20–28 as shown on Thumb chart—70 sts; 11 thumb sts between markers.

Rnd 35: Work in patt to 7 sts before marked thumb sts, then removing thumb markers as you come to them, place the next 18 sts on holder for thumb, use the backward-loop method to CO 8 sts over gap in colors to maintain chart patt, work in patt to end—60 sts rem.

UPPER HAND

Work as for left mitt.

THUMB

Place 18 held thumb sts on dpn and rejoin yarns to end of thumb sts with RS facing. Pick up and knit 8 sts from base of sts CO over thumb gap in colors to match beg of Rnd 35 of left thumb chart, then cont patt over rem 18 sts—26 sts total. Arrange sts as for right thumb and work in patt through Rnd 41 of Left Thumb chart. With A, work ribbing and BO as for right thumb.

FINISHING

Weave in loose ends. Wash in warm soapy water and rinse well. Squeeze out excess moisture, pull to shape, and lay flat to dry. Steam-press gently on WS if desired.

Lilja Textured
JACKET

FINISHED SIZE

About 36½ (41½, 44, 49, 51½)" (92.5 [105.5, 112, 124.5, 131] cm) bust circumference.
Sweater shown measures 44" (112 cm).

YARN

Worsted weight (#4 Medium).
Shown here: Ístex Lett-Lopi (100% wool; 109 yd [100 m]/50 g): #1410 orange, 12 (14, 15, 17, 18) balls.

NEEDLES

Size U.S. 9 (5 mm): 16" and 24" (40 and 60 cm) circular (cir) and set of four double-pointed (dpn). Adjust needle size if necessary to obtain the correct gauge.

NOTIONS

Markers (m); stitch holders; removable markers; size G/6 (4 mm) crochet hook; tapestry needle, three 1" (2.5 cm) buttons.

GAUGE

19 stitches and 38 rows = 4" (10 cm) in tuck stitch pattern; 19 stitches and 25 rows/rounds = 4" (10 cm) in twisted rib patterns.

This elegant jacket, knitted in simple but striking textural stitches with raglan sleeves, is knitted in Lett-Lopi, which, although finer than the Alafoss Lopi, retains all the naturally unique qualities of Icelandic wool. The Lilja Jacket makes a stylish statement and is ideal for wearing both indoors and out.

Lett-Lopi is light, warm, and durable and is available in a range of colors that do justice to Iceland, the island of fire and ice.

NOTES

· The sleeves are worked separately in the round to the underarms, and the lower body is worked in back and forth in rows in one piece to the armholes, then all pieces are arranged on one needle for working the raglan yoke back and forth in rows to the neck edge.

· When working back and forth in rows, slip the first stitch of every RS row knitwise with yarn in back and slip the first stitch of every WS row purlwise with yarn in front.

STITCH GUIDE

TUCK 4 (T4)

Drop next st from needle and ravel it down 4 rows, insert right-hand needle under these 4 loose threads and into the front of the 5th st below the needle, and knit this stitch, catching the loose threads.

TUCK STITCH
(MULTIPLE OF 3 STS + 2)

Set-up row: (WS) Sl 1 (see Notes), k1, *p1, k2; rep from *.

Rows 1 and 3: (RS) Sl 1, p1, *k1, p2; rep from * to last 3 sts, k1, p1, k1.

Rows 2, 4, and 6: Sl 1, k1, *p1, k2; rep from *.

Row 5: Sl 1, p1, *T4 (see above), p2; rep from * to last 3 sts, T4, p1, k1.

Row 6: Rep Row 2.

Rep Rows 1–6 for pattern; do not rep the set-up row.

TWISTED RIB IN THE ROUND
(MULTIPLE OF 3 STS)

All Rnds: P1, *k1 through back loop (tbl), p2; rep from * to last 2 sts, k1tbl, p1.

TWISTED RIB IN ROWS
(MULTIPLE OF 3 STS + 2)

Row 1: (RS) Sl 1, p1, *k1tbl, p2; rep from * to last 3 sts, k1tbl, p1, k1.

Row 2: (WS) Sl l, k1, *p1tbl, k2; rep from *.

Rep Rows 1 and 2 for patt.

FRONT NECK SHAPING

RS Rows: Sl first st as established. If second st on left needle is k1tbl, work next 2 sts tog as k2tog; if second st on left needle is a purl st, work next 2 sts tog as p2tog. Work in patt to last 3 sts. If next st on left needle is k1tbl, work next 2 sts tog as ssk (see Glossary); if next st on left needle is a purl st, work next 2 sts tog as ssp (see Glossary), knit last st—2 sts dec'd, 1 st at each neck edge inside selvedge sts.

WS Rows: Sl first st as established. If second st on left needle is p1tbl, work next 2 sts tog as ssp; if second st on left needle is a knit st, work next 2 sts tog as ssk. Work in patt to last 3 sts. If next st on left needle is p1tbl, work next 2 sts tog as p2tog; if next st on left needle is a knit st, work next 2 sts tog as k2tog, knit last st—2 sts dec'd, 1 st at each neck edge inside selvedge sts.

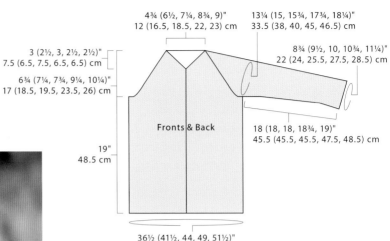

4¾ (6½, 7¼, 8¾, 9)"
12 (16.5, 18.5, 22, 23) cm

13¼ (15, 15¾, 17¾, 18¼)"
33.5 (38, 40, 45, 46.5) cm

3 (2½, 3, 2½, 2½)"
7.5 (6.5, 7.5, 6.5, 6.5) cm

8¾ (9½, 10, 10¾, 11¼)"
22 (24, 25.5, 27.5, 28.5) cm

6¾ (7¼, 7¾, 9¼, 10¼)"
17 (18.5, 19.5, 23.5, 26) cm

Fronts & Back

18 (18, 18, 18¾, 19)"
45.5 (45.5, 45.5, 47.5, 48.5) cm

19"
48.5 cm

36½ (41½, 44, 49, 51½)"
92.5 (105.5, 112, 124.5, 131) cm

Sleeves

With dpn, CO 42 (45, 48, 51, 54) sts. Place marker (pm) and join for working in rnds, being careful not to twist sts. Work twisted rib in the round (see Stitch Guide) until piece measures 3½ (3½, 4, 4, 4)" (9 [9, 10, 10, 10] cm) from CO. Shape sleeve as foll:

Rnd 1: P1, M1pwise (see Glossary), *k1tbl, p2; rep from * to last 2 sts, k1tbl, M1pwise, p1—2 sts inc'd.

Rnds 2–6: *P2, k1tbl; rep from * to last 2 sts, p2.

Rnd 7: P1, M1pwise, *p1, k1tbl, p1; rep from * to last st, M1pwise, p1—2 sts inc'd.

Rnds 8–12: P3, *k1tbl, p2; rep from * to last st, p1.

Rnd 13: P1, M1kwise (see Glossary), *p2, k1tbl; rep from * to last 3 sts, p2, M1kwise, p1— 2 sts inc'd.

Rnds 14–18: P1, *k1tbl, p2; rep from * to last 2 sts, k1tbl, p1.

Rep Rnds 1–18 two (three, three, four, four) more times, changing to shorter cir needle when there are too many sts to fit around dpn—60 (69, 72, 81, 84) sts.

Next rnd: M1kwise, p1, M1pwise, work in patt as established to last st, M1pwise, p1, remove marker, work first 4 sts of rnd again as k1tbl, p2, k1tbl, replace marker—63 (72, 75, 84, 87) sts.

Next rnd: *P2, k1tbl; rep from *.

Rep the last rnd until piece measures 18 (18, 18, 18¾, 19)" (45.5 [45.5, 45.5, 47.5, 48.5] cm) from CO.

Next rnd: Work in patt to last 7 sts, BO 7 sts—56 (65, 68, 77, 80) sts rem; the first 2 and last 2 sts at each end of rem sts should be p2.

Cut yarn and place sts on holder. Make second sleeve in the same manner.

LOWER BODY

With longer cir needle, CO 173 (197, 209, 233, 245) sts. Do not join. Work Rows 1–6 of tuck stitch patt (see Stitch Guide) until piece measures about 17" (43 cm) from CO for all sizes, ending with Row 5 of patt. Beg with Row 2, work even in twisted rib in rows (see Stitch Guide) until piece measures 19" (48.5) from CO for all sizes, ending with RS Row 1.

Next row: (WS) Work 44 (47, 50, 53, 56) sts in patt for left front, BO 7 sts for left armhole, work in patt until there are 71 (89, 95, 113, 119) sts on needle after BO gap for back, BO 7 sts for right armhole, work rem 44 (47, 50, 53, 56) sts in patt for right front—the 2 sts on each side of each armhole gap should be p2.

Leave sts on longer cir needle.

YOKE

Row 1: (RS, joining row) With RS facing and cont in established twisted rib patt, work 43 (46, 49, 52, 55) right front sts, *purl the last body st tog with the first sleeve st and mark this st with a removable marker for raglan by placing the marker in the st itself (and not on the needle between sts), work 54 (63, 66, 75, 78) sleeve sts in patt, purl the last sleeve st tog with the first body st and mark this st with a removable marker for raglan*, work 69 (87, 93, 111, 117) back sts in patt, rep from * to * once more, work 43 (46, 49, 52, 55) left front sts in patt—267 (309, 327, 369, 387) sts total; 43 (46, 49, 52, 55) sts each front; 54 (63, 66, 75, 78) sts each sleeve; 69 (87, 93, 111, 117) back sts; 4 marked raglan sts.

Note: Move the raglan markers up as you work so you can always easily identify the raglan sts.

Row 2: (WS) *Work in established patt to 2 sts before marked st, p2tog, k1 (marked st), ssp (see Glossary); rep from * 3 more times, work in patt to end—8 sts dec'd.

Row 3: *Work in patt to 2 sts before marked st, ssp, p1, p2tog; rep from * 3 more times, work in patt to end—8 sts dec'd.

Row 4: *Work in patt to 2 sts before marked st, k2tog, k1, ssk; rep from * 3 more times, work in patt to end—8 sts dec'd.

Row 5: *Work in patt to 2 sts before marked st, ssk, p1, k2tog; rep from * 3 more times, work in patt to end—8 sts dec'd.

Row 6: Rep Row 4—8 sts dec'd.

Row 7: Rep Row 3—8 sts dec'd.

Row 8: Rep Row 2—211 (253, 271, 313, 331) sts
rem; 36 (39, 42, 45, 48) sts for each front; 40
(49, 52, 61, 64) sts for each sleeve; 55 (73, 79,
97, 103) sts for back; 4 marked raglan sts.

Rows 9, 11, and 13: Work even in patt, working
each marked st as p1—no change to st count.

Rows 10 and 12: Rep Row 4—8 sts dec'd in
each row.

Row 14: Rep Row 2—8 sts dec'd.

Row 15 to Row 24 (30, 30, 42, 48): Rep Rows
9–14 one (two, two, four, five) more time(s),
then work Rows 9–12 once more—147 (165, 183,
177, 171) sts rem; 28 (28, 31, 28, 28) sts for each
front; 24 (27, 30, 27, 24) sts for each sleeve;
39 (51, 57, 63, 63) sts for back; 4 marked raglan
sts; yoke measures about 3¾ (4¾, 4¾, 6¾, 7¾)"
(9.5 [12, 12, 17, 19.5] cm) from joining row.

Row 25 (31, 31, 43, 49) to Row 41 (39, 41, 47, 57):
Note: Front neck shaping (see Stitch Guide)
is worked at the same time as raglan shaping
continues; read the next section through before
proceeding.
Continue to work raglan decs as established
on the next 8 (4, 5, 2, 4) WS rows, then work 1
RS row to end with Row 11 (9, 11, 11, 9) of raglan
shaping. *At the same time* dec 1 st at each neck
edge every row 17 (9, 11, 5, 9) times—49 (115, 121,
151, 121) sts rem; 3 (15, 15, 21, 15) sts for each
front; 8 (19, 20, 23, 16) sts for each sleeve; 23
(43, 47, 59, 55) sts for back; 4 marked raglan sts.
Sizes (41½, 44, 49, 51½)" only: Work (6, 6,
9, 6) more rows, dec 8 sts every row for raglan
shaping as established and dec 1 st at each neck
edge every row—(55, 61, 61, 61) sts rem; 3 sts for
each front for all sizes; (7, 8, 5, 4) sts for each
sleeve; (31, 35, 41, 43) sts for back; 4 marked
raglan sts.

Work (0, 0, 1, 0) row even to end with a RS
row—(45, 47, 57, 63) yoke rows completed.
All sizes: (WS) K3tog, work in patt to last 3
sts, k3tog—45 (51, 57, 57, 57) sts rem; 1 st for
each front for all sizes; no change to other st
counts; 42 (46, 48, 58, 64) yoke rows completed; yoke measures about 6¾ (7¼, 7¾,
9¼, 10¼)" (17 [18.5, 19.5, 23.5, 26] cm) from
joining row.

BO all sts in patt, working each k1tbl as k1 in
BO row.

FINISHING

FRONT FACINGS

With RS facing and beg at transition between
tuck and twisted rib patts, pick up and knit 81
sts for all sizes along the tuck st section of left
front edge (about 3 sts for every 6 rows); do not
pick up along the upper twisted rib section of
the edge. Beg with a WS row, work rev St st (knit
WS rows; purl RS rows) until piece measures 4"
(10 cm). BO all sts. With RS facing and beg at CO
edge of right front, pick up and knit 81 sts for
all sizes along tuck st section of right front edge,
ending at transition between tuck and twisted
rib patts; as for left front, do not pick up along
twisted rib section. Beg with a WS row, work rev
St st until piece measures 4" (10 cm). BO all sts.
Fold each front along the vertical line created
by the drop-st column closest to the edge and
sew the facing invisibly in place around all 3
sides; purl sides of facings will show on inside
of jacket.

FRONT AND NECK EDGING

Note: Jacket shown has button loops on the left front and buttons on the right front, the opposite arrangement from what is typical for women's cardigans.

With crochet hook, RS facing, and beg at lower right front corner, work 1 row of slip-st crochet (see Glossary) to top of right front, across top of sleeves and back neck, and down to lower left front corner, working along the fold line of each faced section. Fasten off last st. Mark position for three buttons on right front, the highest just below start of neck shaping, the lowest just above the transition from tuck to twisted rib, and the rem button centered in between. Joining and breaking off yarn for each loop, work 3 separate short crochet chain (see Glossary) button loops along left front edge opposite each button position.

Weave in loose ends. Press lightly using a warm iron over a damp cloth, being careful not to flatten the texture of the patterns. Sew buttons to right front, opposite button loops.

SHETLAND

Shetland has had a rich association with handknitting for over 500 years. Lying far out in the Atlantic Ocean north of the Scottish mainland, Shetland's northerly position has ensured inclusion in an ancient trade route that stretched from the neighboring Faeroe Islands to Iceland, Norway, Sweden, and beyond to the Baltics. Sheep and wool have always been an integral part of life on Shetland and spinning and wool crafts have been practiced on these islands for thousands of years.

The Shetland sheep produce fleece in a variety of natural shades, and early Shetland knitting would have been made using only these contrasting colors—Shetland black (a very dark brown), Moorit (a lovely rich russet brown), various grays, and white. Later, colorful bands of pattern started to be used to decorate items knitted on Fair Isle, the most southerly of the Shetland Isles. Indigenous lichen and plant dyes, previously only used for dyeing wool for weaving, were used to dye wool intended for knitting. Soft yellows, pale blues, and rosy reds predominated, and traditional Fair Isle colorways and patterning began to evolve. In the early 1800s, newly imported chemical dyes that produced clearer, brighter colors began to replace the local plant dye recipes and distinct new color and pattern combinations that are now universally associated with Fair Isle emerged.

Shetland has always had a harsh, cold, and damp climate, and the success of traditional Fair Isle knitting is owed in no small part to the way it is knitted—seamlessly in the round using the stranded knitting technique. Two colors are used in most rounds of knitting, and the strand not in use is carried across the wrong side and woven as required by the pattern to create a double-thick, dense, durable, and warm fabric ideally suited for protective fisherman's sweaters, caps, and scarves.

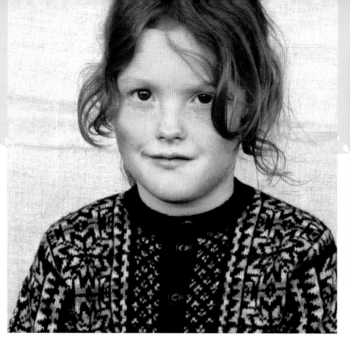

There is much debate regarding the exact origins of the wealth of patterns attributed to early Shetland and Fair Isle knitting, but as was common with the rest of northern Europe, knitted designs were strongly influenced by embroidery and woven designs and ancient "magical" protective symbols. As part of a busy, flourishing trade route, Shetland would easily have been exposed to an inspirational array of exotic textiles and handicrafts from at least as far away as Spain and the Baltics.

Lace knitting in Shetland was probably practiced long before colored, patterned knitting. The Shetland Hap shawl, knitted in natural shades in lace designs, was hugely popular, but the exquisite cobweb fine, lace-knitted shawls traditionally made on Unst, the most northerly of the Shetland Isles, became a fashion sensation. Unst shawls were magnificently patterned, often measuring up to six feet (1.8 meters) square and were so fine and delicate that they could easily pass through a woman's wedding ring. These shawls were handknitted from the finest, softest handspun wool and, despite weighing less than two ounces (57 grams), could take up to two years to complete.

Inspired by the wealth of traditional Shetland knitting techniques, the following five projects are all knitted in superb wool yarns from Jamieson & Smith, who have been producing yarn from the crofters and farmers of Shetland for more than sixty years. Some of the dye recipes have remained unchanged, offering old and unusual shades that produce distinctive and original knits. Fair Isle knitting became very fashionable in the 1920s and 1930s, and I have tried to capture something of this period in each of the garments with patterning, shape, and color. Mostly knitted in the round, the garments are classic, simple, and unfussy, and just as easy to wear today as they have always been.

CROWNING GLORY
COBWEB SHAWL

FINISHED SIZE

About 12½" (31.5 cm) wide and 110"
(279.5 cm) long.

YARN

Laceweight (#0 Lace).
Shown here: Jamieson & Smith 1-Ply Cobweb
(100% wool; 383 yd [350 m]/25 g): natural undyed
white, 6 balls.

NEEDLES

Size U.S. 1 (2.25 mm). Adjust needle size if
necessary to obtain the correct gauge.

NOTIONS

Smooth waste yarn; tapestry needle.

GAUGE

21 stitches and 24 to 25 rows = 2" (5 cm) in
stockinette stitch, after blocking; exact gauge is
not critical for this project.

This truly magnificent lace shawl is steeped in
Shetland tradition—the intricate stitch patterns have
been passed down from one generation to the next,
and the wool is of the finest quality.

Jamieson & Smith's traditional 1-ply Cobweb-
weight yarn, spun from the fleece of the native
Shetland sheep, is as light and delicate as a cobweb,
and just as beautiful. Surely, this Crowning Glory
Cobweb Shawl is fit for royal Finn Folk or Selkie
princesses.

NOTES

· The scarf is worked in two halves from the ends toward the center, then the live sts of the two pieces are grafted together.

· Because the waste yarn used for stitch holders will remain in place during washing and blocking, make sure to use a colorfast yarn that will not stain the scarf.

STITCH GUIDE

BOBBLE

Work ([k1, yo] 2 times, k1) all in same st—5 sts made from 1 st. Turn work, k5, turn work, p5, turn work, ssk, k1, k2tog—3 sts rem. Turn work, p3tog—1 st rem.

P2TOGB

(WS) P1, return this st to left-hand needle, insert right-hand needle into second st and lift it over the purl st and off the needle, then return the purl st to the right-hand needle—1 st dec'd; this makes a left-leaning dec when viewed from the RS.

SL 2, K1, P2SSO

Sl 2 sts individually knitwise, k1, pass the 2 slipped sts over the knit st—2 sts dec'd; this makes a left-leaning double dec with the first slipped st on top.

VERTICAL LACE STRIPES

(MULTIPLE OF 5 STS + 4)

Row 1: (RS) K2, yo, ssk, *k1, k2tog, [yo] 2 times, ssk; rep from * to last 5 sts, k1, k2tog, yo, k2.

Row 2: P6, *work (p1, k1) in double yo of previous row, p3; rep from * to last 3 sts, p3.

Rep Rows 1 and 2 for pattern.

CROWN OF GLORY

(MULTIPLE OF 14 STS + 5, DEC'D TO MULTIPLE OF 8 STS + 5)

Row 1: (RS) K3, *ssk, k9, k2tog, k1; rep from * to last 2 sts, k2—patt has dec'd to a multiple of 12 sts + 5.

Row 2: (WS) P2, *p1, p2tog, p7, p2togb (see at left); rep from * to last 3 sts, p3—patt has dec'd to a multiple of 10 sts + 5.

Row 3: K3, *ssk, k2, [yo] 3 times, k3, k2tog, k1; rep from * to last 2 sts, k2—patt has inc'd to a multiple of 11 sts + 5, counting each triple yo as 3 sts.

Row 4: P2, *p1, p2tog, p2, work ([k1, p1] 2 times, k1) all in triple yo of previous row, p1, p2togb; rep from * to last 3 sts, p3—st count rems unchanged.

Row 5: K3, *ssk, k6, k2tog, k1; rep from * to last 2 sts, k2—patt has dec'd to a multiple of 9 sts + 5.

Row 6: P2, *p1, p2tog, p6; rep from * to last 3 sts, p3—patt has dec'd to a multiple of 8 sts + 5.

Row 7: K3, *k1, [yo, k1] 6 times, k1; rep from * to last 2 sts, k2—patt has inc'd to a multiple of 14 sts + 5 again.

Rows 8 and 10: Purl.

Row 9: Knit

Row 11: K2, *k2tog, yo; rep from * to last 3 sts, k3.

Rows 12–14: Rep Rows 8–10.

Rep Rows 1–14 for pattern.

SCARF FIRST HALF

Loosely CO 131 sts.

Set-up row: (WS) Purl.

Rows 1 (RS)–97: Work Rows 1–14 of Crown of Glory patt (see Stitch Guide) 6 times, then work Rows 1–13 once more.

Row 98: P1, [p32, M1 pwise (see Glossary)] 3 times, p34—134 sts.

Rows 99–110: Work Rows 1 and 2 of Vertical Lace Stripes patt (see Stitch Guide) 6 times.

Row 111: Knit.

Row 112: P1, [p31, p2tog] 3 times, p34—131 sts rem.

Row 113: K2, *k2tog, yo; rep from * to last 3 sts, k3.

Rows 114–119: Work 6 rows even in St st, ending with a RS row.

Rows 120–145: Work WS set-up row of Coronet chart, then work Rows 1–25 once.

Rows 146–150: Work 5 rows even in St st, beg and end with a WS row.

Row 151: K2, *k2tog, yo; rep from * to last 3 sts, k3.

Row 152: Purl.

Row 153: Knit.

Rows 154–169: Rep Rows 98–113—134 sts after completing Row 154 (same as Row 98), and 131 sts after completing Row 168 (same as Row 112).

CORONET

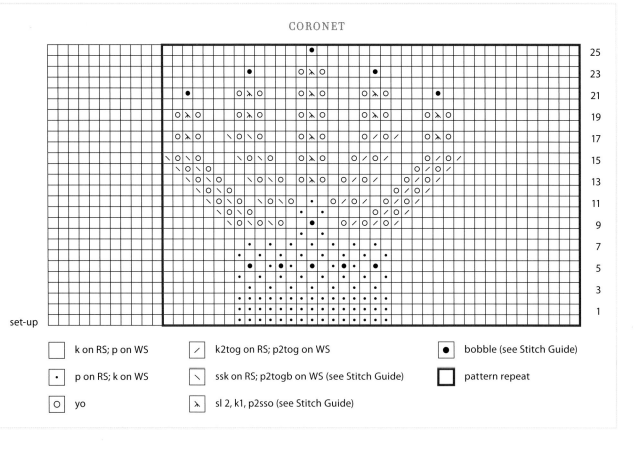

	k on RS; p on WS		/	k2tog on RS; p2tog on WS		●	bobble (see Stitch Guide)
●	p on RS; k on WS		\	ssk on RS; p2togb on WS (see Stitch Guide)			pattern repeat
○	yo		⋏	sl 2, k1, p2sso (see Stitch Guide)			

Rows 170–172: Work 3 rows even in St st, beg
  and end with a WS row.
Rep Rows 1–172 three more times—689 rows
total, including set-up row. Break yarn. Place sts
on smooth waste yarn holder.

Scarf Second Half

Cast on 131 sts. Work Rows 1–172 three times as
for first half, then work Rows 1–148 once, ending
with a WS row 3 rows after last Coronet chart
row—665 rows total, including set-up row. Place
sts on smooth waste yarn holder. Break yarn,
leaving a tail about 3 times the width of the scarf
for grafting.

Finishing

Wash the pieces according to the ball band direc-
tions, roll in a towel to remove excess moisture,
then block the pieces to about 12½" (31.5 cm)
wide, 56" (142 cm) long for the first half, and 54"
(137 cm) long for the second half. Allow pieces to
air-dry completely.

Return live sts to the needles if you find it easier
to graft that way, and with long tail threaded on
a tapestry needle, use the Kitchener stitch (see
Glossary) to graft, matching the tension of the
surrounding fabric. The vertical lace stripes
section at the end of the first half will be in the
center of the scarf. Weave in loose ends.

MOTH
SHORT-SLEEVED TOP

FINISHED SIZE

33½ (37, 40, 44½, 48)" (85 [94, 101.5, 113, 122] cm) bust circumference.
Sweater shown measures 40" (101.5 cm).

YARN

Laceweight (#0 Lace).
Shown here: Jamieson & Smith 2-Ply Lace Weight (100% wool; 252 yd [230 m]/25 g): #L5 dark brown (A), 2 (2, 3, 3, 3) balls; #L54 dark gray (B), #L27 medium gray (C), #L203 light gray (D), and #L1A cream (E), 2 (2, 2, 2, 3) balls each.

NEEDLES

Size 3 mm (no exact U.S. equivalent; between U.S. sizes 2 and 3): straight and 16" (40 cm) circular (cir) or set of 4 double-pointed (dpn). Adjust needle size if necessary to obtain the correct gauge.

NOTIONS

Tapestry needle; two ¾" (2 cm) decorative buttons.

GAUGE

30 stitches and 56 rows = 4" (10 cm) in striped garter-rib pattern.

Jamieson & Smith's Shetland 2-ply lace yarn is truly wonderful to work with. It is naturally soft (a touch of lambswool is added), light as a feather, warm, and cosseting. The naturally earthy colors and simple garter-rib pattern combine perfectly to make this pullover a delicate classic knit. The pattern is reminiscent of the markings on a moth's wings, and the style is slightly retro.

Moth is easily worn under a jacket or cardigan or, with its little capped sleeves and pretty vintage buttons, it is sweet enough to wear just on its own.

STITCH GUIDE

STRIPED GARTER RIB
(MULTIPLE OF 6 STS + 3)

Rows 1 (RS) and 2 (WS): With A, *k3, p3; rep from * to last 3 sts, k3.

Rows 3 and 4: With B, rep Row 1.

Rows 5 and 6: With C, rep Row 1.

Rows 7 and 8: With D, rep Row 1.

Rows 9 and 10: With E, rep Row 1.

Rep Rows 1–10 for patt.

BACK

With A and straight needles, CO 135 (147, 159, 177, 189) sts. Work in striped garter-rib patt (see Stitch Guide) for 40 (40, 40, 50, 50) rows, ending with Row 10 of patt. *Dec 1 st each end of needle on next RS row, work 19 (29, 29, 19, 29) rows even; rep from * 3 (2, 2, 3, 2) more times, then dec 1 st each end of needle on foll RS row—125 (139, 151, 167, 181) sts rem. Work even in patt until 130 (140, 140, 140, 150) rows have been completed, ending with Row 10 of patt—piece measures 9¼ (10, 10, 10, 10¾)" (23.5 (25.5, 25.5, 25.5, 27.5] cm) from CO.

SHAPE ARMHOLES

BO 4 (5, 5, 6, 7) sts at beg of next 2 rows—117 (129, 141, 155, 167) sts rem. Dec 1 st each end of needle every row 4 (4, 6, 8, 10) times, then every other row 3 (4, 5, 5, 6) times—103 (113, 119, 129, 135) sts rem. Work even in patt until 231 (241, 245, 261, 275) rows have been completed from CO, ending with Row 1 (1, 5, 1, 5) of patt—armholes measure 7¼ (7¼, 7½, 8½, 9)" (18.5 [18.5, 19, 21.5, 23] cm).

SHAPE NECK AND SHOULDERS

Next row: (WS, Row 2 [2,6,2,6] of patt) Work 35 (38, 40, 45, 48) sts in patt, join new yarn and BO center 33 (37, 39, 39, 39) sts, work in patt to end—35 (38, 40, 45, 48) sts each side.

Working each side separately, at each neck edge BO 5 sts 2 times, then BO 3 (3, 3, 3, 4) sts once and *at the same time* at each armhole edge BO 7 (8, 9, 11, 11) sts 2 times, then BO 8 (9, 9, 10, 12) sts once—no sts rem.

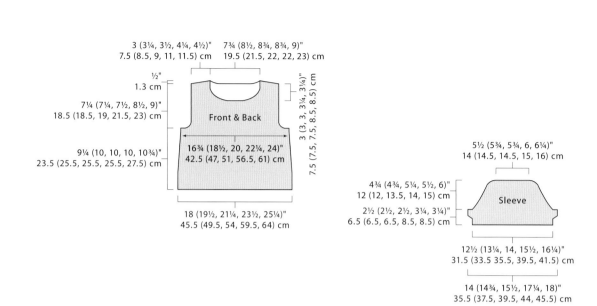

3 (3¼, 3½, 4¼, 4½)"
7.5 (8.5, 9, 11, 11.5) cm

7¾ (8½, 8¾, 8¾, 9)"
19.5 (21.5, 22, 22, 23) cm

½"
1.3 cm

7¼ (7¼, 7½, 8½, 9)"
18.5 (18.5, 19, 21.5, 23) cm

Front & Back

3 (3, 3, 3¼, 3¼)"
7.5 (7.5, 7.5, 8.5, 8.5) cm

9¼ (10, 10, 10, 10¾)"
23.5 (25.5, 25.5, 25.5, 27.5) cm

16¾ (18½, 20, 22¼, 24)"
42.5 (47, 51, 56.5, 61) cm

18 (19½, 21¼, 23½, 25¼)"
45.5 (49.5, 54, 59.5, 64) cm

5½ (5¾, 5¾, 6, 6¼)"
14 (14.5, 14.5, 15, 16) cm

4¾ (4¾, 5¼, 5½, 6)"
12 (12, 13.5, 14, 15) cm

Sleeve

2½ (2½, 2½, 3¼, 3¼)"
6.5 (6.5, 6.5, 8.5, 8.5) cm

12½ (13¼, 14, 15½, 16¼)"
31.5 (33.5 35.5, 39.5, 41.5) cm

14 (14¾, 15½, 17¼, 18)"
35.5 (37.5, 39.5, 44, 45.5) cm

Front

Work as for back until 189 (199, 201, 215, 231) rows have been completed from beg, ending with Row 9 (9, 1, 5, 1) of patt—103 (113, 119, 129, 135) sts; armholes measure 4¼ (4¼, 4½, 5¼, 5¾)" (11 [11, 11.5, 13.5, 14.5] cm).

SHAPE NECK

Next row: (WS, Row 10 [10,2,6,2] of patt) Work 43 (47, 50, 55, 57) sts in patt, join new yarn and BO center 17 (19, 19, 19, 21) sts, work in patt to end—43 (47, 50, 55, 57) sts each side.
Working each side separately, at each neck edge BO 3 sts 2 times, then BO 2 sts 5 times—27 (31, 34, 39, 41) sts rem. Dec 1 st at each neck edge every RS row 3 (4, 5, 5, 5) times, then every other RS row 2 times—22 (25, 27, 32, 34) sts rem. Work even in patt until 231 (241, 245, 261, 275) rows

have been completed from CO, ending with Row 1 (1, 5, 1, 5) of patt—armholes measure 7¼ (7¼, 7½, 8½, 9)" (18.5 [18.5, 19, 21.5, 23] cm).

SHAPE SHOULDERS

At each armhole edge BO 7 (8, 9, 11, 11) sts 2 times, then BO 8 (9, 9, 10, 12) sts once—no sts rem.

Sleeves

With A and straight needles, CO 93 (99, 105, 117, 123) sts. Work 10 rows in k1, p1 rib, ending with a WS row—piece measures about 1" (2.5 cm). Change to striped garter-rib patt, and inc 1 st each end of needle every row 6 times, working new sts into patt—105 (111, 117, 129, 135) sts.

Work 14 (14, 14, 24, 24) rows even, ending with Row 10 of patt—piece measures 2½ (2½, 2½, 3¼, 3¼)" (6.5 [6.5, 6.5, 8.5, 8.5] cm) from CO.

SHAPE CAP

BO 4 (5, 5, 6, 7) sts at beg of next 2 rows—97 (101, 107, 117, 121) sts rem. Dec 1 st each end of needle every row 4 (4, 6, 8, 10) times, then every other row 8 (10, 10, 12, 8) times, then every 4th row 10 (9, 10, 10, 13) times—53 (55, 55, 57, 59) sts rem. BO 3 sts at beg of next 4 rows—41 (43, 43, 45, 47) sts rem. BO all sts.

FINISHING

NECKBAND

With MC threaded on a tapestry needle, sew shoulder seams. Place waste yarn markers on each side of the center 3 sts from the 17 (19, 19, 19, 21) sts BO at front neck. With A, cir needle or dpn, RS facing, and starting at marker after the 3 marked sts, pick up and knit 47 (49, 50, 52, 53) sts along right front neck, 63 (67, 69, 69, 71) sts across back neck, and 47 (49, 50, 52, 53) sts along left front neck, ending at marker before the 3 marked sts—157 (165, 169, 173, 177) sts total. Do not join. Work back and forth in rows as foll:

Row 1: (WS) K1, *p1, k1; rep from * to end.
Row 2: (RS) K1, *k1, p1; rep from * to last 2 sts, k2.
Rep these 2 rows 4 more times, then work Row 1 once more—11 rows total. BO all sts in patt.

With MC threaded on a tapestry needle, sew side and sleeve seams. Sew sleeve caps into armholes, easing to fit. Weave in loose ends. Press lightly using a warm iron over a damp cloth, taking care not to flatten the pattern texture. Sew a button on each side of split neckband at center front.

Effie
FAIR ISLE PULLOVER

FINISHED SIZE

35½ (40½, 45½, 50½)" (90 [103, 115.5, 128.5] cm)
bust circumference.
Sweater shown measures 40½" (103 cm).

YARN

Fingering (#1 Super Fine).
Shown here: Jamieson & Smith 2-Ply Jumper Weight
(100% wool; 130 yd [119 m]/25 g): #54 dark gray
(A), #203 light gray (C), #FC43 sand (H), #121
yellow (J), and #125 dark orange (L), 3 (3, 4, 4) balls
each; #93 bright red (E) and #202 beige (G), 2 balls
each; #27 medium gray (B), #FC6 pink (D), #1403
dark red (F), #FC7 peach (K), #75 pale turquoise
(M), and #14 light blue (N), 1 ball each.

NEEDLES

Size U.S. 3 (3.25 mm): 16" and 32" (40 and 80 cm)
circular and set of 4 or 5 double-pointed (dpn).
Adjust needle size if necessary to obtain the
correct gauge.

NOTIONS

Markers (m); stitch holders; tapestry needle.

GAUGE

30 stitches and 34 rounds/rows = 4" (10 cm) in
charted color patterns.

Effie is an elegant example of a contemporary Fair
Isle Sweater. The vibrant, rich colors of Jamieson
& Smith's pure wool 2-ply jumper yarn (there
are more than eighty shades!) have been used on
Shetland to knit traditional Fair Isle sweaters for
decades. Here, a combination of thirteen shades,
with brights working alongside softer, muted tones,
give the ancient Shetland OXO pattern its distinctive
classic look.

NOTES

· The lower body is worked in the round, then
the back and front are worked separately, back
and forth in rows, to the shoulders. The sleeves
are worked in the round from the cuffs upward,
then sewn into the armholes during finishing.

· When working in the round, read all chart rows
as RS rounds. When working back and forth
in rows, odd-numbered rows are RS rows and
even-numbered rows are WS rows.

· Color B does not appear in the symbol key
because it is only used for the ribbed edgings,
not in the charted pattern.

Stitch Guide

POCKETS (MAKE 2)

With J and shorter cir needle or 2 dpn, CO
31 sts. Work in St st for 20 rows. Place sts on
holder. Make a second pocket the same as
the first.

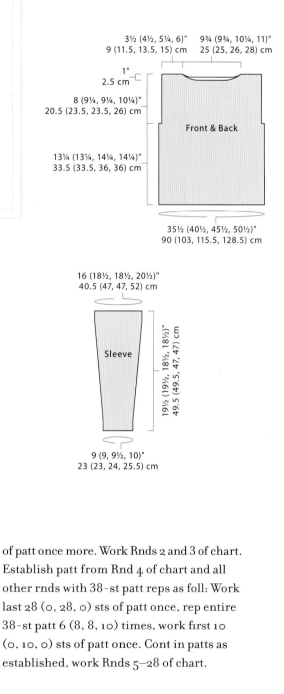

Body

With A and longer cir needle, CO 264 (304,
340, 380) sts. Place marker (pm) and join
for working in rnds, being careful not to
twist sts; rnd begins at left side at start of
front sts. Work rib as foll:

Rnds 1–3: *K3 with A, p1 with B; rep from *.

Rnds 4–6: *K3 with A, p1 with C; rep from *.

Rnds 7–9: *K3 with A, p1 with D; rep from *.

Rnds 10–12: Rep Rnds 4–6.

Rnds 13–15: Rep Rnds 1–3, inc 2 (0, 2, 0) sts
   in last rnd—266 (304, 342, 380) sts; piece
   measures about 1¾" (4.5 cm) from CO.
Establish patt from Rnd 1 of Effie chart (see
page 62) and all other rnds with 4-st patt
reps as foll: Work 4-st patt rep 66 (76, 85, 95)
times around, then work first 2 (0, 2, 0) sts

of patt once more. Work Rnds 2 and 3 of chart.
Establish patt from Rnd 4 of chart and all
other rnds with 38-st patt reps as foll: Work
last 28 (0, 28, 0) sts of patt once, rep entire
38-st patt 6 (8, 8, 10) times, work first 10
(0, 10, 0) sts of patt once. Cont in patts as
established, work Rnds 5–28 of chart.

EFFIE, RNDS 1–46

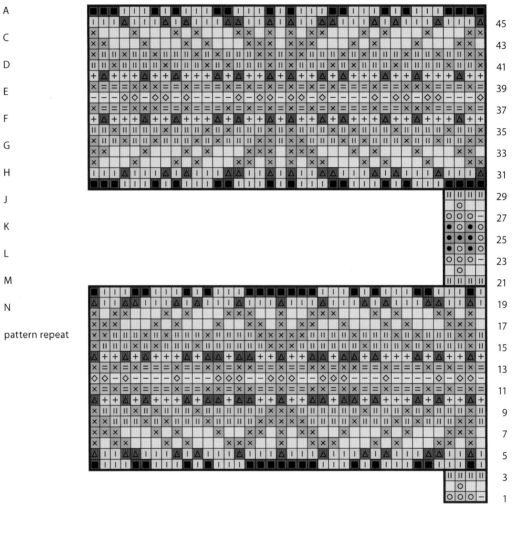

Legend:
- ● A
- ○ C
- – D
- △ E
- ■ F
- I G
- H
- II J
- ◇ K
- × L
- = M
- + N
- ☐ pattern repeat

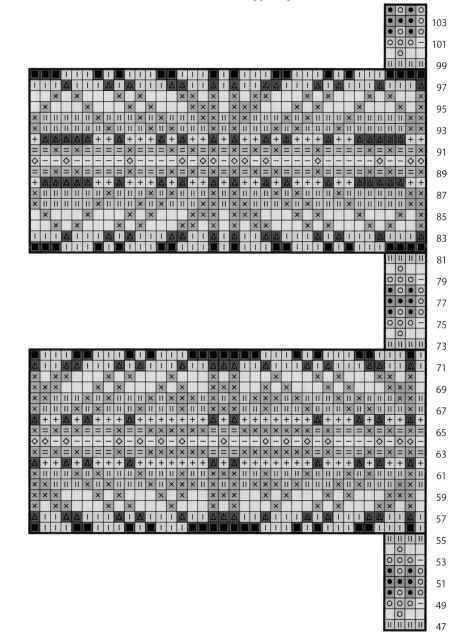

INSERT POCKETS

Next rnd: (Rnd 29 of chart) With J, k13 (23, 32, 42),
*place next 31 sts on holder, place 31 held
pocket sts on left-hand needle with RS facing,
knit across 31 pocket sts*, k45 for all sizes,
rep from * to * once more for second pocket,
knit to end.

Work in patt until Rnd 98 of chart has been
completed, then work 0 (0, 8, 8) more rnds to
end with Rnd 98 (98, 2, 2) of chart—piece
measures about 13¼ (13¼, 14¼, 14¼" (33.5
[33.5, 36, 36] cm) from CO.

DIVIDE FOR ARMHOLES

(RS Rnd 99 (99, 3, 3) of chart) With J, BO 4 (6, 8,
10) sts, work in patt until there are 125 (141, 155,
171) front sts after BO, BO 8 (11, 16, 19) sts, work
in patt to last 4 (5, 8, 9) sts, BO 4 (5, 8, 9) sts,
break yarns—125 (141, 155, 171) sts each for front
and back. Place 125 (141, 155, 171) back sts on
holder (the side of lower body without pockets).

FRONT

Rejoin yarns to 125 (141, 155, 171) front sts with
WS facing, ready to work Row 100 (100, 4, 4)
of chart as a WS row. Working back and forth in
rows, work in patt until Row 54 (64, 72, 80) has
been completed.

SHAPE NECK

(RS Row 55 [65, 73, 81] of chart) Work 45 (53, 58,
64) sts in patt for left front neck, then place rem
80 (88, 97, 107) sts on holder or allow sts to rest
on needle while shaping left front neck.

Cont in patt on sts of left front only, at beg of
WS rows BO 8 sts once, then BO 6 sts once, then

BO 3 sts once, then BO 2 sts once, then work 1
row even to end with RS Row 63 (73, 81, 89) of
chart—26 (34, 39, 45) sts rem; armhole measures about 8 (9¼, 9¼, 10¼)" (20.5 [23.5, 23.5,
26] cm). Place sts on holder for left shoulder.
Place center 35 (35, 39, 43) sts on separate holder
for front neck. Return 45 (53, 58, 64) right front
neck sts to needle if they are not already on the
needle and rejoin yarns with RS facing, ready to
work Row 55 (65, 73, 81) of chart. Cont in patt, at
beg of RS rows BO 8 sts once, then BO 6 sts once,
then BO 3 sts once, then BO 2 sts once, then
work 2 rows even to end with Row 63 (73, 81, 89)
of chart—26 (34, 39, 45) sts rem. Place sts on
holder for right shoulder.

BACK

Return 125 (141, 155, 171) held back sts to longer
cir needle and rejoin yarns with WS facing, ready
to work Row 100 (100, 4, 4) of chart as a WS row.
Working back and forth in rows, work in patt
until Row 58 (68, 76, 84) has been completed.

SHAPE NECK

(RS Row 59 (69, 77, 85) of chart) Work 36 (44,
49, 55) sts in patt for right back neck, then place
rem 89 (97, 106, 116) sts on holder or allow sts to
rest on needle while shaping right back neck.

Cont in patt on sts of right back only, BO 5 sts at
beg of next 2 WS rows, then work 1 row even to
end with RS Row 63 (73, 81, 89) of chart—
26 (34, 39, 45) sts rem; armhole measures about
8 (9¼, 9¼, 10¼)" (20.5 [23.5, 23.5, 26] cm).
Place sts on holder for right shoulder. Place center 53 (53, 57, 61) sts on separate holder for back
neck. Return 36 (44, 49, 55) left front neck sts to

needle if they are not already on the needle and rejoin yarns with RS facing, ready to work Row 59 (69, 77, 85) of chart. Cont in patt, BO at beg of 5 sts at beg of next 2 RS rows, then work 2 rows even to end with Row 63 (73, 81, 89) of chart—26 (34, 39, 45) sts rem. Place sts on holder for left shoulder.

SLEEVES

With A and dpn, CO 68 (68, 72, 76) sts. Pm and join for working in rnds, being careful not to twist sts. Work Rnds 1–15 of rib as for body, inc 1 st at end of Rnd 15—69 (69, 73, 77) sts.

Establish patt from Rnd 1 of Effie chart as foll: Work last st of patt once, then rep entire 4-st patt to end. Work Rnds 2 and 3 of chart. Establish patt from Rnd 4 of chart as foll: Work last 15 (15, 17, 19) sts of patt once, work entire 38-st patt once, then work first 16 (16, 18, 20) sts of patt once. Cont in patts as established and *at the same time* beg on Rnd 5 of chart, inc 1 st each side of marker every 5 (4, 4, 4) rnds 26 (35, 33, 28) times, then every 0 (0, 0, 2) rnds 0 (0, 0, 10) times, working new sts into chart patt and changing to shorter cir needle when there are too many sts to fit on dpn—121 (139, 139, 153) sts. Work even in patt until Rnd 46 (46, 38, 38) of chart has been completed—150 (150, 142, 142) chart rnds total; piece measures 19½ (19½, 18½,

18½)" (49.5 [49.5, 47, 47] cm) from CO. *Note:* The larger sizes have increasingly wider upper bodies, so they have shorter sleeves to prevent the cuff-to-cuff "wingspan" of the sweater from becoming too wide. BO all sts.

FINISHING

NECKBAND
With J threaded on a tapestry needle, use the Kitchener st (see Glossary) to graft the shoulder sts tog. With A, shorter cir needle, and RS facing, pick up and knit 23 sts along left front neck, k35 (35, 39, 43) held front neck sts, pick up and knit 23 sts along right front neck, 11 sts along right back neck, k53 (53, 57, 61) held back neck sts, then pick up and knit 11 sts along left back neck—156 (156, 164, 172) sts total. Pm and join for working in rnds. Work Rnds 1–9 of rib as for body. With A, work in k3, p1 rib for 6 rnds. BO all sts. Fold neckband in half and, with A threaded on a tapestry needle, invisibly whip-stitch (see Glossary) BO edge of neckband to WS of pick-up rnd.

POCKETS
Return 31 held pocket sts to needle and rejoin J with WS facing. Purl 1 WS row, then BO all sts kwise with RS facing. Slip-stitch short ends of trim at top of pocket to RS of front, then sew sides and bottom of pocket lining invisibly on WS. Rep for other pocket.

Weave in loose ends. With J threaded on a tapestry needle, sew sleeves into armholes, easing to fit. Press lightly using a warm iron over a damp cloth.

NELL SHETLAND
CAP

FINISHED SIZE

About 19" (48.5 cm) head circumference; will stretch to fit about 22" (56 cm).

YARN

Fingering weight (#1 Super Fine).
Shown here: Jamieson & Smith 2-Ply Jumper Weight (100% wool; 130 yd [119 m]/25 g): #1403 deep red (A), #FC6 soft pink (B), #121 soft yellow (C), #118 deep green (D), and #75 turquoise (E), 1 ball each.

NEEDLES

Hat: Size U.S. 2 (2.75 mm): set of 4 double-pointed (dpn). *Ribbing:* Size U.S. 1 (2.25 mm): set of 4 dpn. Adjust needle size if necessary to obtain the correct gauge.

NOTIONS

Marker (m); tapestry needle.

GAUGE

15 stitches and 21 rounds = 2" (5 cm) in solid-color stockinette stitch on larger needles, worked in rounds; 15 stitches and 17 rounds = 2" (5 cm) in stockinette colorwork section from chart on larger needles, worked in rounds.

This sweet, simple cap is knitted from the top down and incorporates both a peerie pattern and a classic Shetland border pattern. Inspired by the vast array of vintage, traditionally knitted and patterned hats once worn as everyday wear on Shetland, this little cap is knitted in Jamieson & Smith's traditional 2-ply jumper yarn and is ideally suited to keeping your head warm in the worst of fogs or the strongest of gales. Simple embroidery stitches provide extra dashes of color.

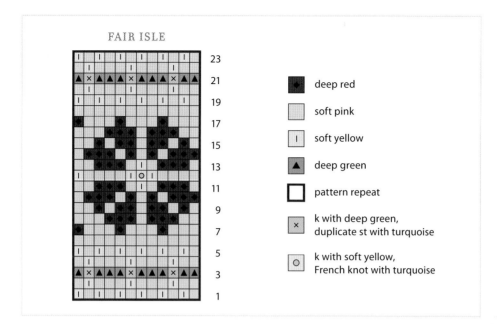

FAIR ISLE

	deep red
	soft pink
	soft yellow
	deep green
	pattern repeat
	k with deep green, duplicate st with turquoise
	k with soft yellow, French knot with turquoise

HAT

With A and larger needles, CO 6 sts. Divide sts evenly on 3 dpn (2 sts each needle), place marker (pm), and join for working in rnds.

Rnd 1: Knit as tightly as possible.

Rnd 2: *K1f&b; rep from *—12 sts.

Rnd 3 and all odd-numbered rnds: Knit.

Rnd 4: *K1, k1f&b; rep from *—18 sts.

Rnd 6: *K2, k1f&b; rep from *—24 sts.

Rnd 8: *K3, k1f&b; rep from *—30 sts.

Cont to inc 6 sts every even-numbered rnd in this manner, working 1 more st between incs on each inc rnd until there are 144 sts (48 sts on each needle).

Knit 2 rnds even—piece measures about 4½" (11.5 cm). Break off A. Work Rnds 1–23 of Fair Isle chart. Rejoin A and knit 2 rnds even—piece measures about 7½" (19 cm) from beg.

Next rnd: *K22, ssk; rep from *—138 sts rem.

Next rnd: *K21, ssk; rep from *—132 sts rem.

Next rnd: *K20, ssk; rep from *—126 sts rem.

Next rnd: Change to smaller needles, *k2, p2; rep from * to last 2 sts, end k2; because the number of sts is not an even multiple of 4 sts, all rib rnds will begin and end with k2.

Rep the last rnd 3 more times. Change to B and work 1 rnd in rib as established. BO all sts in rib patt.

FINISHING

Weave in loose ends. With turquoise, work duplicate stitch and French knots (see Glossary for embroidery instructions) as indicated on chart. Block lightly.

HESTER CHEVRON
LACE PULLOVER

FINISHED SIZE

About 32¾ (37¾, 42¾, 47¾, 52¾)" (83 [96, 108.5, 121.5, 134] cm) bust circumference.
Sweater shown measures 42¾" (108.5 cm).

YARN

Fingering (#1 Super Fine).
Shown here: Jamieson & Smith 2-ply Jumper Weight (100% wool; 125 yd [114 m]/25 g): #118 green (MC), 5 (6, 7, 8, 9) balls; #029 teal (A), #125 orange (B), #FC7 orange heather (C), #121 gold (D), #FC43 tan (E), #075 light blue (F), and #1403 dark red (G), 2 balls each for all sizes.

NEEDLES

Size U.S. 3 (3.25 mm): straight and 16" and 32" (40 and 80 cm) circular (cir). Adjust needle size if necessary to obtain the correct gauge.

NOTIONS

Marker; tapestry needle; one 1⅛" (2.9 cm) decorative button.

GAUGE

27 stitches and 37 rows = 4" (10 cm) in stockinette stitch; 2 pattern repeats wide (34 to 42 stitches) and 36 rounds (9 patt reps high) measure 5" (12.5 cm) wide and 4" (10 cm) high in chevron lace patt, worked in rounds.

Inspired by marvelous old photos from the 1920s of lady walkers in Shetland, this loose-fitting pullover makes good use of the Dimple Shale and Rib stitch, which is a variation of the Old Shale pattern used in classic Shetland lace. With its scalloped edge and dainty details, this stitch is reminiscent of foamy, gently breaking waves on a beach.

Knitted in Jamieson & Smith's traditional 2-ply jumper yarn, this pullover is ideal for both indoor and outdoor wear. The range of colors available in this yarn is absolutely wonderful with some of the dye recipes having remained unchanged for decades.

NOTES

- The lower body and sleeves are worked in the round in striped chevron lace pattern. The upper back and fronts are worked separately in rows in solid-color stockinette.

- The chevron lace pattern is worked by repeating the same 4 pattern rounds over and over, but the colors are changed according to the stripe sequences given in the Stitch Guide. For example, when the lower body stripe sequence says, "work 8 rnds MC; *2 rnds each A, B, C, D, E, F, and G," that means to work the first 8 rounds using MC, then continue the pattern as established using the colors A, B, C, D, E, F, and G (in that order), changing colors every 2 rounds.

- To reduce the number of ends to weave in, do not cut the yarn after each stripe. Instead, let the unused stripe colors hang out of the way on the WS of the work, bringing them up into position when they are needed again.

- The lower body and sleeves are planned to have the same length for all sizes. To increase length, work additional rounds in stockinette with MC after finishing the chevron lace pattern, but before dividing for the back and fronts on the lower body or before binding off for the sleeves. Plan on purchasing extra MC if making a longer version. For shorter pieces, eliminate some of the stripe rounds from the end of the chevron pattern before finishing the pattern with a few rounds of MC. Every 9 rounds added or removed will lengthen or shorten the piece by about 1" (2.5 cm).

Stitch Guide

CHEVRON LACE

(MULTIPLE OF 17 STS, INC'D
TO MULTIPLE OF 21 STS)

Rnd 1: *K2, p2, ssk, [k1, yo] 6 times, k1, k2tog,
  p2; rep from *—patt has inc'd to a multiple
  of 21 sts.

Rnd 2: *K2, p2, k15, p2; rep from *.

Rnd 3: *K2, p2, k3tog tbl, k9, k3tog, p2; rep from *
  —patt has dec'd to a multiple of 17 sts again.

Rnd 4: *K2, p2, k11, p2; rep from *.

Rep Rnds 1–4 for patt.

STRIPE SEQUENCES

Lower body: Work 8 rnds MC; *2 rnds each A,
  B, C, D, E, F, and G; 2 rnds MC; 2 rnds each A,
  B, C, D, E, F, and G,** [1 rnd each MC, A, B, C,
  D, E, F, and G] 2 times, 2 rnds MC;* rep the 48
  rnds from * to * once more, then work the 30
  rnds from * to ** once more, then work 5 rnds
  MC—139 rnds total.

Sleeve: Work 8 rnds MC; rep the 48 rnds from *
  to * as for lower body 3 times, then work 3 rnds
  MC—155 rnds total.

5¼ (6½, 7½, 8¾, 9¾)"   5¾ (5¾, 6¼, 6¼, 7)"
13.5 (16.5, 19, 22, 25) cm   14.5 (14.5, 16, 16, 18) cm

8 (8½, 9, 9½, 10)"
20.5 (21.5, 23, 24, 25.5) cm

Front & Back

15½"
39.5 cm

32¾ (37¾, 42¾, 47¾, 52¾)"
83 (96, 108.5, 121.5, 134) cm

Sleeve

17¼"
44 cm

17¾ (17¾, 20, 20, 20)"
45 (45, 51, 51, 51) cm

Body

With MC and longer cir needle, loosely CO 221
(255, 289, 323, 357) sts. Place marker (pm) and
join for working in rnds, begin careful not to
twist sts. Work in chevron lace patt (see Stitch
Guide) for 139 rounds, ending with Rnd 3 of patt
and changing colors according to the lower body
stripe sequence (see Stitch Guide and Notes)—
piece measures about 15½" (39.5 cm) from CO
for all sizes.

DIVIDE BACK & FRONTS

With MC and straight needles, k99 (116, 133,
150, 167), turn, purl back across 99 (116, 133,
150, 167) sts just worked, remove end-of-rnd
marker, purl the next 12 (11, 12, 11, 12) sts—111

(127, 145, 161, 179) back sts on straight needles; allow the rem 110 (128, 144, 162, 178) front sts to rest on cir needle while working the back.

BACK

Working St st back and forth in rows with MC, work even until piece measures 8 (8½, 9, 9½, 10)" (20.5 [21.5, 23, 24, 25.5] cm) from dividing row, ending with a WS row. BO all sts.

LEFT FRONT

With RS facing, rejoin MC to beg of 110 (128, 144, 162, 178) front sts on cir needle at left armhole edge.

Next row: (RS) K52 (61, 69, 78, 86), k2tog, k1, turn—54 (63, 71, 80, 88) left front sts; allow rem 55 (64, 72, 81, 89) right front sts to rest on cir needle while working left front.

Work 3 rows even in St st, beg and ending with a WS row.

Dec row: (RS) Knit to last 3 sts, k2tog, k1—1 st dec'd at neck edge.

Cont in St st, rep the shaping of the last 4 rows 17 (18, 19, 20, 21) more times—36 (44, 51, 59, 66) sts rem. Work even until piece measures 8 (8½, 9, 9½, 10)" (20.5 [21.5, 23, 24, 25.5] cm) from dividing row, ending with a WS row. BO all sts.

RIGHT FRONT

With RS facing, rejoin MC to beg of rem 55 (64, 72, 81, 89) right front sts on cir needle at right neck edge.

Dec row: (RS) K1, ssk, knit to end—1 st dec'd. Work 3 rows even in St st, beg and ending with a WS row. Cont in St st, rep the shaping of the last 4 rows 17 (18, 19, 20, 21) more times, then work 1 more RS dec row—36 (44, 51, 59, 66) sts rem. Work even until piece measures 8 (8½, 9, 9½, 10)" (20.5 [21.5, 23, 24, 25.5] cm) from dividing row, ending with a WS row. BO all sts.

SLEEVES

With MC and shorter cir needle, loosely CO 119 (119, 136, 136, 136) sts. Pm and join for working in rnds, begin careful not to twist sts. Work in chevron lace patt for 155 rnds, ending with Rnd 3 of patt and changing colors according to the sleeve stripe sequence (see Stitch Guide and Notes)—piece measures about 17¼" (44 cm) from CO for all sizes. BO all sts with MC.

FINISHING

NECK EDGING

With yarn threaded on a tapestry needle, sew fronts to back at shoulders. With MC, longer cir needle, RS facing, and beg at base of V-neck, pick up and knit 59 (63, 67, 70, 74) sts along right front neck, 39 (39, 43, 43, 47) sts across back neck, and 59 (63, 67, 70, 74) sts along left front neck—157 (165, 177, 183, 195) sts total. Do not join. Knit 1 WS row. BO all sts kwise on next RS row.

With yarn threaded on a tapestry needle, sew sleeves into armholes, easing to fit and matching the chevron patt k2 column closest to the center of the sleeve to the shoulder seam.

Weave in loose ends. Press lightly with a warm iron over a damp cloth. Sew decorative button in place at base of V-neck as shown.

HESTER CHEVRON LACE PULLOVER

NORWAY

Norwegian folk art and handicrafts have always been influenced by the daily routine of rural life. The mountainous landscapes, with vast distances of fjords, lakes, and forests, created whole areas that were often totally isolated, and for rural communities with no means to travel, home became the center of life. Stark differences in the natural world and the extreme contrast between summer and winter led to the Norwegian sense of color and form, and a vast wealth of handicrafts in every district, each with unique details and features.

Knitting has existed in Norway since at least the 1500s and was an integral part of everyday peasant life, with both the old and young knitting essential items such as mittens and caps to keep them warm through the harsh winters while working outdoors and in the forests. The patterned, stranded Norwegian skiwear we are familiar with today did not become fashionable or widely used until the mid 1800s. Bright colorful fisherman's sweaters (knitted in reds, blues, and whites and patterned with stars, checks, and bands of lice stitch) were made at this time in Fana, but the most distinctive of all of Norway's folk knitting from this period is the *lusekofte*. These fine black wool jerseys, which originated in an isolated southern valley of Norway in the 1860s, were patterned all over with white lice stitches and featured embroidered black fabric edgings and decorative buttons.

A young peasant woman named Marit Emstad knitted the first pair of white wool mittens patterned with black wool stars in the 1850s. This now-famous type of patterning is named for her home in Selbu, a small northerly district of Norway. Marit also adapted patterns from other crafts, such as embroidery and weaving, to establish many of the patterns so closely associated with Norwegian knitwear today—reindeer, moose, stars, snowflakes, and rows of dancing people.

By the end of the 1800s, industrialization had changed the country's economic structure and communications improved as towns and cities grew. Attempts to transfer folk crafts to machinery failed and, as a result, cheap, inferior, imported goods predominated. In a bid to create a new, modern style of handicrafts, attempts were made to unite the new industrialized world with the old folk traditions. In 1918, a group of designers, artists, and craftsmen set up the *Brukskunst* (the Applied Art Association). The *Brukskunst* proclaimed that everything needed for everyday life should be well designed and beautifully made, and consequently, traditional styles and methods were preserved and inspired future generations.

In 1953, knitwear designer Unn Søiland Dale founded Lillunn Design of Norway with the intention of renewing interest in traditional Norwegian knitting techniques, patterns, and yarns. Her first sweaters were sold in Paris and London. She later collaborated with French fashion houses Dior and Givenchy, and her designs were often featured in *Vogue*. Unn Søiland Dale successfully secured the brightly colored Norwegian ski sweater its place in knitwear history.

Inspired by the wonderfully patterned Norwegian knitwear from the 1940s and 1950s and traditional Norwegian textiles and costumes, I have designed five projects that are as beautiful and useful today as they were in the past. Dale of Norway has produced high-quality woolen yarn for well over a hundred years; and their classic, pure Norwegian wool Heilo yarn has been in production since 1938. I hope that the use of authentic woolen yarn, folk patterns, and traditional techniques will help perpetuate Norwegian folk art traditions.

ANNEMOR
PULLOVER

FINISHED SIZE

34¼ (38¾, 43¼, 47, 51¾)" (87 [98.5, 110, 119.5, 131.5] cm) bust circumference.
Sweater shown measures 43¼" (110 cm).

YARN

Sportweight (#2 Fine).
Shown here: Dale of Norway Heilo (100% wool; 109/50 g): #0007 gray (MC), 12 (13, 14, 16, 17) balls; #0020 cream (CC), 2 (2, 3, 3, 3) balls; #5813 light blue (EC), small amount for embroidery.

NEEDLES

Size U.S. 5 (3.75 mm): 16" and 32" (40 and 80 cm) circular (cir) and set of 4 or 5 double-pointed (dpn). Adjust needle size if necessary to obtain the correct gauge.

NOTIONS

Markers (m); stitch holder; tapestry needle.

GAUGE

26 stitches and 32 rows/rounds = 4" (10 cm) in stockinette stitch.

Annemor is a classic turtleneck sweater inspired by the wonderful and varied designs of the traditional Norwegian *lusekofte*, the lice-stitch patterns and large stars that are so synonymous with Norwegian knitting today. Annemor is knitted in just two colors with subtle highlights added with duplicate stitch.

Knitted in Dale of Norway's pure wool Heilo yarn, this sweater is ideal for outdoor wear, especially when snow falls.

NOTES

- The lower body is worked in the round, then the upper front and back are worked separately, back and forth in rows, to the shoulders. The sleeves are worked in the round from the cuffs upward, then sewn into the armholes during finishing.

- When working in the round, read all chart rows as RS rounds. When working back and forth in rows, odd-numbered rows are RS rows, and even-numbered rows are WS rows.

- When working the Snowflake chart, strand the contrasting color (CC) all the way to the selvedges.

- Although the lower part of the sleeve is worked in the round, the sleeve is drawn opened out flat on the schematic to show the shape of the sleeve cap.

STITCH GUIDE

K2, P2 RIB
(MULITPLE OF 4 STS)
All rnds: *K2, p2; rep from *.

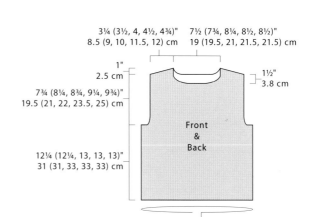

3¼ (3½, 4, 4½, 4¾)"   7½ (7¾, 8¼, 8½, 8½)"
8.5 (9, 10, 11.5, 12) cm   19 (19.5, 21, 21.5, 21.5) cm

1"
2.5 cm

1½"
3.8 cm

7¾ (8¼, 8¾, 9¼, 9¾)"
19.5 (21, 22, 23.5, 25) cm

Front & Back

12¼ (12¼, 13, 13, 13)"
31 (31, 33, 33, 33) cm

34¼ (38¾, 43¼, 47, 51¾)"
87 (98.5, 110, 119.5, 131.5) cm

BODY

With MC and longer cir needle, CO 216 (240, 264, 288, 312) sts. Place marker (pm) and join for working in rnds, being careful not to twist sts. Work in k2, p2 rib (see Stitch Guide) until piece measures 1¾" (4.5 cm).

Next rnd: *K1f&b, k26 (19, 15, 13, 12), k1f&b, k26 (19, 16, 13, 12); rep from * to last 0 (0, 0, 8, 0) sts, k0 (0, 0, 8, 0)—224 (252, 280, 308, 336) sts. Knit 1 rnd with MC. Work Rnds 1–5 of Diamonds chart (see page 83), beg and ending where indicated for body. Knit 4 rnds with MC.

Next rnd: Knit, dec 2 (dec 0, inc 2, dec 2, dec 0) sts evenly spaced—222 (252, 282, 306, 336) sts. Work in patt from Lice chart, beg and ending where indicated for body, until piece measures about 12¼ (12¼, 13, 13, 13)" (31 [31, 33, 33, 33] cm) from CO, ending with Rnd 1 or 7 of chart.

3¼ (3½, 4½, 5, 5¾)"
8.5 (9, 11.5, 12.5, 14.5) cm

4¼ (4¾, 4¾, 5, 5¼)"
11 (12, 12, 12.5, 13.5) cm

Sleeve

18½ (19, 19½, 19½, 19½)"
47 (48.5, 49.5, 49.5, 49.5) cm

13 (13¾, 15¼, 16¼, 17¾)"
33 (35, 38.5, 41.5, 45) cm

9¾ (9¾, 9¾, 10¾, 10¾)"
25 (25, 25, 27.5, 27.5) cm

Dividing rnd: (Rnd 2 or 8 of chart) With MC, BO 12 (13, 14, 18, 19) sts for left armhole, knit until there are 99 (113, 127, 135, 149) front sts on needle after BO gap, place sts just worked on holder, BO 12 (13, 14, 18, 19) sts for right armhole, knit to end—99 (113, 127, 135, 149) back sts rem.

BACK

Working St st back and forth in rows with MC only, purl 1 WS row, then dec 1 at each side on the next 2 RS rows—95 (109, 123, 131, 145) sts rem.

Next row: (WS) P3 (10, 17, 21, 28), pm, p89, pm, p3 (10, 17, 21, 28).

Next row: (RS) Dec 1 st at armhole edge, knit to m, slip m (sl m), work Row 1 of Snowflake chart over center 89 sts, sl m, knit to end dec 1 st at armhole edge—93 (107, 121, 129, 143) sts rem.

Working sts on each side of chart in St st with MC, cont in patt and *at the same time* dec 1 st at each armhole edge on next 1 (5, 8, 8, 13) RS row(s)—91 (97, 105, 113, 117) sts rem. Cont even in patt until Row 29 of chart has been completed. Work even in St st with MC only until armholes measure 7¾ (8¼, 8¾, 9¼, 9¾)" (19.5 [21, 22, 23.5, 25] cm), ending with a WS row.

SHAPE BACK NECK AND SHOULDERS

Next row: (RS) K31 (33, 36, 39, 41), join new yarn and BO center 29 (31, 33, 35, 35) sts, knit to end—31 (33, 36, 39, 41) sts rem each side.

Working each side separately, at each neck edge BO 5 sts 2 times and *at the same time* for shoulder shaping, at each armhole edge BO 7 (8, 9, 10, 11) sts 2 times, then BO 7 (7, 8, 9, 9) sts once—no sts rem.

FRONT

Return 99 (113, 127, 135, 149) held front sts to longer cir needle. Beg with MC and WS facing, work as for back until armholes measure 6¼ (6¾, 7¼, 7¾, 8¼)" (16 [17, 18.5, 19.5, 21] cm), ending with a WS row—91 (97, 105, 113, 117) sts rem.

SHAPE FRONT NECK AND SHOULDERS

(RS) K36 (39, 42, 46, 48), join new yarn and BO center 19 (19, 21, 21, 21) sts, knit to end—36 (39, 42, 46, 48) sts rem each side.

Working each side separately, at each neck edge BO 5 (6, 6, 6, 6) sts once, then BO 5 (5, 5, 6, 6) sts once, then BO 3 sts once, then BO 2 sts once—21 (23, 26, 29, 31) sts rem each side. Work even in St st until armholes measure 7¾ (8¼, 8¾, 9¼, 9¾)" (19.5 [21, 22, 23.5, 25] cm), ending with a WS row. At each armhole edge BO 7 (8, 9, 10, 11) sts 2 times, then BO 7 (7, 8, 9, 9) sts once—no sts rem.

SNOWFLAKE

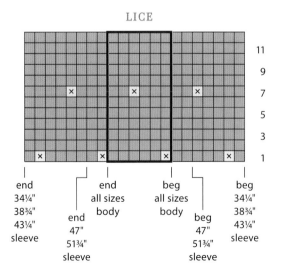

29
27
25
23
21
19
17
15
13
11
9
7
5
3
1

	k with MC on all rnds and RS rows; p with MC on WS rows			St st with MC, duplicate st with EC
×	k with CC on all rnds and RS rows; p with CC on WS rows			pattern repeat

LICE

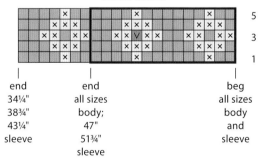

11
9
7
5
3
1

end
34¼"
38¾"
43¼"
sleeve

end
47"
51¾"
sleeve

end
all sizes
body

beg
all sizes
body

beg
47"
51¾"
sleeve

beg
34¼"
38¾"
43¼"
sleeve

DIAMONDS

5
3
1

end
34¼"
38¾"
43¼"
sleeve

end
all sizes
body;
47"
51¾"
sleeve

beg
all sizes
body
and
sleeve

SLEEVES

With MC and dpn, CO 56 (56, 56, 64, 64) sts. Pm and join for working in rnds, being careful not to twist sts. Work in k2, p2 rib until piece measures 3½" (9 cm).

Next rnd: *K7 (7, 7, 9, 9), k1f&b; rep from * to last 0 (0, 0, 4, 4) sts, k0 (0, 0, 4, 4)—63 (63, 63, 70, 70) sts.

Knit 1 rnd. Work Rnds 1–5 of Diamonds chart, beg and ending where indicated for your size. Knit 4 rnds with MC.

Work Rnds 1–3 of Lice chart, beg and ending where indicated for your size.

Inc rnd: K1f&b with MC, work in patt to last 2 sts, k1f&b with MC, k1 MC—2 sts inc'd.

Cont in patt, rep inc rnd every 9 (8, 6, 6, 4) rnds 10 (12, 17, 17, 22) more times, working new sts into chart patt and changing to shorter cir needle when there are too many sts to fit around dpn—85 (89, 99, 106, 116) sts. Work even in patt until piece measures about 18½ (19, 19½, 19½, 19½)" (47 [48.5, 49.5, 49.5, 49.5] cm) from CO, ending with Rnd 6 or 12 of chart and ending last rnd 6 (6, 7, 9, 9) sts before end-of-rnd m.

Next rnd: With MC, BO 12 (13, 14, 18, 19) sts, removing end-of-rnd m as you come to it, knit to end—73 (76, 85, 88, 97) sts rem.

SHAPE CAP

Working St st back and forth in rows with MC only, purl 1 WS row. Cont in St st, dec 1 st each end of needle on the next 4 rows, then on the next 10 (13, 12, 14, 14) RS rows—45 (42, 53, 52, 61) sts rem. Dec 1 st each end of needle on the next 6 (4, 6, 4, 6) rows—33 (34, 41, 44, 49) sts rem. BO 3 sts at beg of the next 4 rows—21 (22, 29, 32, 37) sts rem. BO all sts.

FINISHING

NECKBAND

With MC threaded on a tapestry needle, sew shoulder seams. With MC, shorter cir needle, RS facing, and beg at left shoulder seam, pick up and knit 61 (63, 65, 67, 67) sts across front neck and 51 (53, 55, 57, 57) sts across back neck—112 (116, 120, 124, 124) sts total. Work in k2, p2 rib for 6¼" (16 cm). BO all sts in patt.

Sew sleeves into armholes. Weave in loose ends. Press lightly using a warm iron over a damp cloth.

THORA CARDIGAN

FINISHED SIZE

32½ (37½, 42½, 47½, 52½)" (82.5 [95, 108, 120.5, 133.5] cm) bust circumference, including 1" (2.5 cm) for front bands.
Sweater shown measures 42½" (108 cm).

YARN

Sportweight (#2 Fine).
Shown here: Dale of Norway Heilo (100% wool; 109/50 g): #0083 dark gray (A), 7 (8, 9, 10, 11) balls; #0004 light gray (B) and #4018 red (C), 2 (3, 3, 3, 4) balls each; and #0020 cream (D), 1 (2, 2, 2, 2) ball(s).

NEEDLES

Size U.S. 2 (3 mm): 16" and 32" (40 and 60 cm) circular (cir) and two sets of 4 double-pointed (dpn). Adjust needle size if necessary to obtain the correct gauge.

NOTIONS

Stitch holders; smooth, contrasting waste yarn for holders; stitch markers; tapestry needle; seven Norwegian clasps about 2" (5 cm) wide when clasped.

GAUGE

24 sts and 30 rows/rounds = 4" (10 cm) in solid-color stockinette; 55 rows/rounds of Charts 1, 2, and 3 together measure 7¾" (19.5 cm) high.

Since the 1950s, bright colors and bold patterning have been the mainstay of Norwegian knitwear, and skiwear in particular. Thora is a classic-styled cardigan inspired by this relatively new tradition. The bands of patterns that include birds, zigzags, and stylized leaves and flowers, are all inspired by Norwegian embroideries and are steeped in folk traditions.

Knitted in Dale of Norway's naturally insulating pure wool Heilo yarn, this cardigan makes ideal skiwear, of course!

NOTES

- The body is worked back and forth in rows in one piece to the armholes, then the upper back and fronts are worked separately.

- The sleeves are worked in the round from the cuff upward, then joined to live stitches picked up around the armhole openings.

- In Chart 1, work the individual bird and leaf motifs using the intarsia method with a separate strand or butterfly of B or C for each motif. If the beginning or ending point for your size will cut off part of a bird or leaf, do not work a partial motif. Work the stitches in stockinette with A instead.

- In Rows/Rounds 5–20 of Chart 3, work each leaf motif using the intarsia method and a separate strand of C and work each 1-stitch vertical line in intarsia with a separate strand of A.

- To customize the lower body length, work more or fewer plain stockinette rows before working the dividing row. To customize sleeve length, work more or fewer plain stockinette rounds after the last sleeve increase and before starting Chart 1 on the upper sleeve. Every 8 rows/rounds added or removed will lengthen or shorten the piece by about 1" (2.5 cm).

STITCH GUIDE

TWISTED RIB IN ROWS
(EVEN NUMBER OF STS)

Row 1: (RS) *K1 through back loop (tbl), p1;
    rep from *.

Row 2: *K1, p1 tbl; rep from *.

Rep Rows 1 and 2 for patt.

TWISTED RIB IN ROUNDS
(EVEN NUMBER OF STS)

All rnds: *K1 tbl, p1; rep from *.

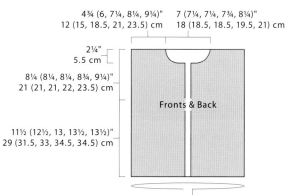

4¾ (6, 7¼, 8¼, 9¼)"
12 (15, 18.5, 21, 23.5) cm

7 (7¼, 7¼, 7¾, 8¼)"
18 (18.5, 18.5, 19.5, 21) cm

2¼"
5.5 cm

8¼ (8¼, 8¼, 8¾, 9¼)"
21 (21, 21, 22, 23.5) cm

11½ (12½, 13, 13½, 13½)"
29 (31.5, 33, 34.5, 34.5) cm

Fronts & Back

32½ (37½, 42½, 47½, 52½)"
82.5 (95, 108, 120.5, 133.5) cm

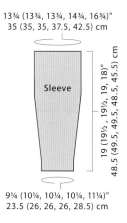

13¾ (13¾, 13¾, 14¾, 16¾)"
35 (35, 35, 37.5, 42.5) cm

Sleeve

19 (19½, 19½, 19, 18)"
48.5 (49.5, 49.5, 48.5, 45.5) cm

9¼ (10¼, 10¼, 10¼, 11¼)"
23.5 (26, 26, 26, 28.5) cm

FLORAL BORDER

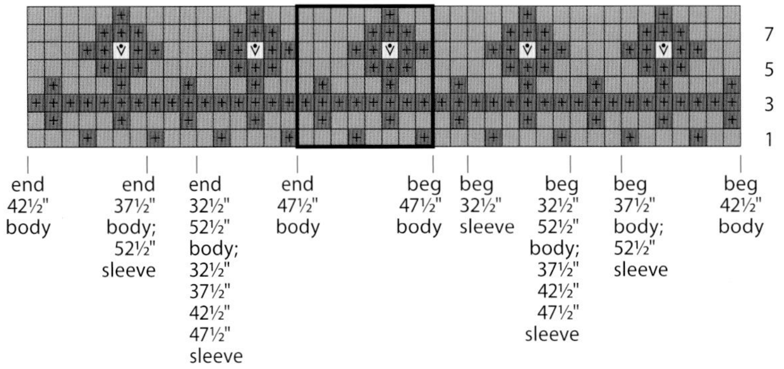

7
5
3
1

end
42½"
body

end
37½"
body;
52½"
sleeve

end
32½"
52½"
body;
32½"
37½"
42½"
47½"
sleeve

end
47½"
body

beg
47½"
body

beg
32½"
sleeve

beg
32½"
52½"
body;
37½"
42½"
47½"
sleeve

beg
37½"
body;
52½"
sleeve

beg
42½"
body

☐ k with A on all rnds and RS rows;
p with A on WS rows

⊠ k with B on all rnds and RS rows;
p with B on WS rows

⊞ k with C on all rnds and RS rows;
p with C on WS rows

⊡ k with D on all rnds and RS rows;
p with D on WS rows

Ⅴ St st with A, duplicate st with C

Ⅴ St st with A, duplicate st with D

☐ pattern repeat

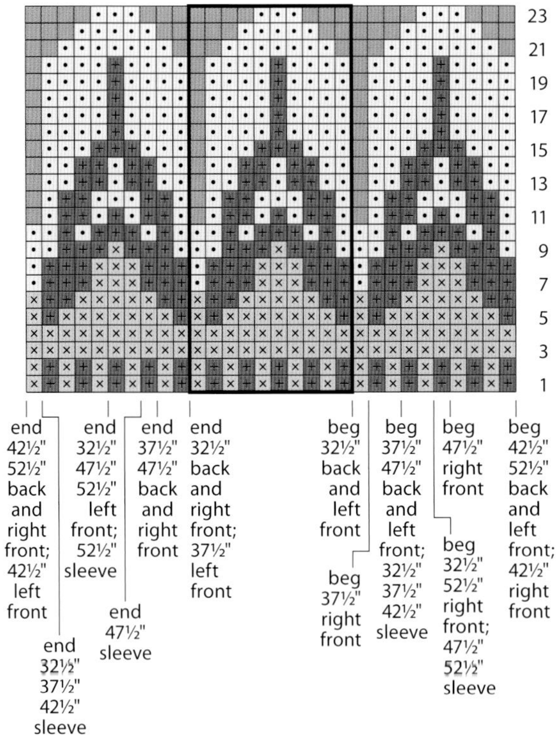

CHART 3

23
21
19
17
15
13
11
9
7
5
3
1

end
42½"
52½"
back
and
right
front;
42½"
left
front

end
32½"
47½"
52½"
left
front;
52½"
sleeve

end
37½"
47½"
back
and
right
front

end
32½"
back
and
right
front;
37½"
left
front

end
47½"
sleeve

end
32½"
37½"
42½"
sleeve

beg
32½"
back
and
left
front

beg
37½"
right
front

beg
37½"
47½"
back
and
left
front;
32½"
37½"
42½"
sleeve

beg
47½"
right
front

beg
32½"
52½"
right
front;
47½"
52½"
sleeve

beg
42½"
52½"
back
and
left
front;
42½"
right
front

CHART 1

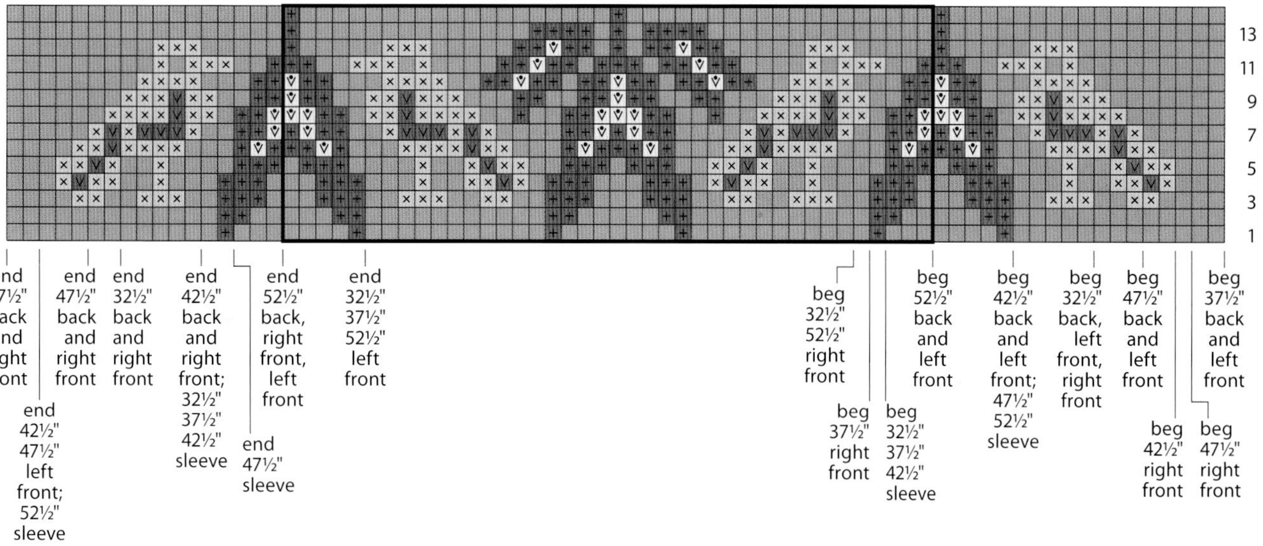

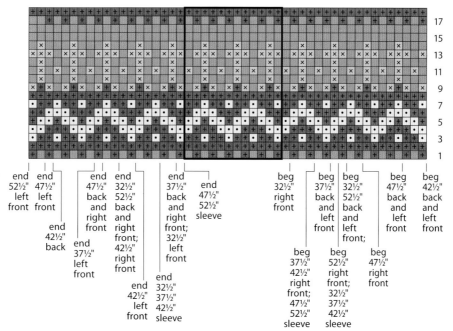

13
11
9
7
5
3
1

end 37½" back and right front
end 42½" 47½" left front; 52½" sleeve

end 47½" back and right front

end 32½" back and right front

end 42½" back and right front; 32½" 37½" 42½" sleeve

end 52½" back, right front, left front
end 47½" sleeve

end 32½" 37½" 52½" left front

beg 32½" 52½" right front
beg 37½" right front

beg 52½" back and left front

beg 42½" back and left front; 47½" 52½" sleeve

beg 32½" back, left front, right front

beg 47½" back and left front
beg 42½" right front

beg 37½" back and left front
beg 47½" right front

CHART 2

17
15
13
11
9
7
5
3
1

end 52½" left front

end 47½" left front
end 42½" back

end 47½" back and right front
end 37½" left front

end 32½" 52½" back and right front; 42½" right front

end 42½" left front
end 32½" 37½" 42½" sleeve

end 37½" back and right front; 32½" left front

end 47½" 52½" sleeve

beg 32½" right front

beg 37½" back and left front
beg 37½" 42½" right front; 47½" 52½" sleeve

beg 32½" 52½" back and left front;
beg 52½" right front; 32½" 37½" 42½" sleeve

beg 47½" back and left front
beg 47½" right front

beg 42½" back and left front

BODY

With A and longer cir needle, CO 160 (184, 210, 234, 260) sts. Do not join. Work in twisted rib in rows (see Stitch Guide) for 12 rows, inc 0 (1,0,1,0) st in last row—160 (185,210,235,260) sts; piece measures 1¾" (4.5 cm).

Next row: (RS) K10, M1 (see Glossary), *k5, M1; rep from * to last 5 sts, k5—190 (220, 250, 280, 310) sts.

Purl 1 WS row. Work Rows 1-8 of Floral Border chart (see page 90), beg and ending where indicated for your size—piece measures about 3" (7.5 cm) from CO. Cont even in St st with A until piece measures 11½ (12½, 13, 13½, 13½)" (29 [31.5, 33, 34.5, 34.5] cm) from CO or desired length to armholes (see Notes), ending with a WS row.

Dividing row: (RS) K45 (52, 60, 67, 75) and *at the same time* inc 0 (1, 0, 1, 0) st and place the 45 (53, 60, 68, 75) sts just worked on a holder for right front, k100 (115, 130, 145, 160) for back, place rem 45 (53, 60, 68, 75) sts for left front on a separate holder—100 (115, 130, 145, 160) back sts rem.

BACK

Work 1 (1, 1, 5, 9) row(s) in St st with A, beg and ending with a WS row.

Beg and ending where indicated for your size, work Rows 1–14 of Chart 1, then Rows 1–18 of Chart 2, then Rows 1–23 of Chart 3. With A, work 2 rows in St st, ending with a RS row—piece measures 8¼ (8¼, 8¼, 8¾, 9¼)" (21 [21, 21, 22, 23.5] cm) from dividing row. Place 29 (36, 43, 49, 55) sts at each side on separate holders for shoulders, then place rem 42 (43, 44, 47, 50) sts on another holder for center back neck.

RIGHT FRONT

Return 45 (53, 60, 68, 75) held right front sts to longer cir needle and rejoin A with WS facing. Work 1 (1, 1, 5, 9) row(s) in St st with A, beg and ending with a WS row.

Next row: (RS) Establish patt from Row 1 of Chart 1 as foll: Work 0 (0, 15, 16, 0) sts before patt rep once, work last 35 (36, 0, 0, 35) sts of patt rep once, work entire 40-st patt 0 (0, 1, 1, 1) time, work 10 (17, 5, 12, 0) sts after patt rep once.

Cont in patt as established, work Rows 2–14 of Chart 1. Beg and ending where indicated for your size, work Rows 1–18 of Chart 2, then Rows 1–10 of Chart 3.

SHAPE NECK

Row 11: (RS) Work first 5 (5, 5, 6, 7) sts in patt, place sts just worked on waste yarn holder, work in patt to end—40 (48, 55, 62, 68) sts rem.

Even-Numbered Rows 12–22: Work even in patt.

Row 13: Work first 4 (5, 5, 6, 6) sts in patt, place sts just worked on same waste yarn holder, work in patt to end—36 (43, 50, 56, 62) sts rem.

Rows 15 and 17: Work first 2 sts in patt, place sts just worked on same holder, work in patt to end—32 (39, 46, 52, 58) sts rem after Row 17.

Rows 19, 21, and 23: Work 1 st in patt, place st just worked on same holder, work in patt to end—29 (36, 43, 49, 55) shoulder sts rem after Row 21; 16 (17, 17, 19, 20) neck sts on holder.

With A, work 2 rows in St st, ending with a RS row—piece measures 8¼ (8¼, 8¼, 8¾, 9¼)" (21 [21, 21, 22, 23.5] cm) from dividing row. Place shoulder sts on separate holder.

LEFT FRONT

Return 45 (53, 60, 68, 75) held left front sts to longer cir needle and rejoin A with RS facing. Work 2 (2, 2, 6, 10) row in St st with A, ending with a WS row.

Next row: (RS) Establish patt from Row 1 of Chart 1 as foll: Work 10 (18, 5, 13, 0) sts before patt rep once, work first 35 (35, 0, 0, 0) sts of patt rep once, work entire 40-st patt 0 (0, 1, 1, 1) time, work 0 (0, 15, 15, 0) sts after patt rep once, then for size 52½" (133.5 cm) only, work first 35 sts of patt rep once more.

Cont in patt as established, work Rows 2–14 of Chart 1. Beg and ending where indicated for your size, work Rows 1–18 of Chart 2, then Rows 1–9 of Chart 3.

SHAPE NECK

Row 10: (WS) Work first 5 (5, 5, 6, 7) sts in patt, place sts just worked on waste yarn holder, work in patt to end—40 (48, 55, 62, 68) sts rem.

Odd-Numbered Rows 11–21: Work even in patt.

Row 12: Work first 4 (5, 5, 6, 6) sts in patt, place sts just worked on same holder, work in patt to end—36 (43, 50, 56, 62) sts rem.

Rows 14 and 16: Work first 2 sts in patt, place sts just worked on same holder, work in patt to end—32 (39, 46, 52, 58) sts rem after Row 16.

Rows 18, 20, and 22: Work 1 st in patt, place st just worked on same holder, work in patt to end—29 (36, 43, 49, 55) shoulder sts rem after Row 22; 16 (17, 17, 19, 20) neck sts on holder.

Row 23: Work even in patt.

With A, work 2 rows in St st, ending with a RS row—piece measures 8¼ (8¼, 8¼, 8¾, 9¼)" (21 [21, 21, 22, 23.5] cm) from dividing row. Place shoulder sts on separate holder.

EMBROIDERY

Work duplicate stitch embroidery (see Glossary) shown on charts as foll using appropriate colored yarn threaded on a tapestry needle. For Floral Border charts, work single-stitch flower centers of Row 6 with D. On Chart 1, work accents in center of each leaf motif with D and work details on each bird motif with C.

JOIN SHOULDERS

Place held right shoulder sts of front and back on separate dpn and hold pieces tog with WS touching and RS facing outward. With A and another dpn, use the three-needle method (see Glossary) to join shoulder sts tog; the bind-off will form a decorative welt on the outside of the garment. Join left shoulder sts in the same manner.

SLEEVES

With A and dpn, CO 46 (52, 52, 52, 56) sts. Place marker (pm) and join for working in rnds, being careful not to twist sts. Work in twisted rib in rnds (see Stitch Guide) for 12 rnds, inc 1 (0,0,0,1) st in last rnd—47 (52,52,52,57) sts; piece measures 1¾" (4.5 cm).

Next rnd: K1, *M1, k5; rep from *, to last 6 sts, M1, k6—56 (62, 62, 62, 68) sts.

Knit 1 rnd. Work Rnds 1–8 of Floral Border chart, beg and ending where indicated for your size—piece measures about 3" (7.5 cm) from CO. Cont in St st with A as foll:

Inc rnd: K1, M1, knit to last st, M1, k1—2 sts inc'd. Knit 2 rnds. *Rep inc rnd, then knit 4 (4, 4, 3, 2) rnds; rep from * 9 (6, 6, 9, 12) more times—78 (78, 78, 84, 96) sts. Work inc rnd, knit 4 (9, 9, 9, 4) rnds, work inc rnd once more, changing to shorter cir needle when there are too many sts to fit around dpn—82 (82, 82, 88, 100) sts. Work even in St st with A until piece measures 11 (11½, 11½, 11, 10)" (28 [29, 29, 28, 25.5] cm) from CO. *Note:* The larger sizes have increasingly wider upper bodies, so they have shorter sleeves to prevent the cuff-to-cuff "wingspan" of the sweater from becoming too wide.

Next row: (RS) Establish patt from Row 1 of Chart 1 as foll: Work 0 (0, 0, 5, 5) sts before patt rep once, work last 37 (37, 37, 0, 0) sts of patt rep once, work entire 40-st patt 1 (1, 1, 2, 2) time(s), work 5 (5, 5, 3, 15) sts after patt rep once. Cont in patt as established, work Rows 2–14 of Chart 1. Beg and ending where indicated for your size, work Rows 1–18 of Chart 2, then Rows 1–23 of Chart 3. With A, work 2 rows in St st, ending with a RS row—piece measures 19 (19½, 19½, 19, 18)" (48.5 [49.5, 49.5, 48.5, 45.5] cm) from CO. Leave sts on needle.

JOIN SLEEVE

With A, RS facing, using as many dpn as necessary, and beg at base of armhole opening, pick up and knit 82 (82, 82, 88, 100) sts evenly around armhole; 41 (41, 41, 44, 50) sts on each side of shoulder join. Pm and join for working in rnds. Knit 2 rnds. Hold live sleeve sts and sts picked up around armhole tog with WS touching and RS facing outward, taking care to match the center of the live sleeve sts to the shoulder join and the shaping line sleeve "seam" to the base of the armhole. With A and another dpn, use the three-needle method to join sleeve and armhole sts; the bind-off will form a decorative welt on the outside of the garment. Work the second sleeve the same as the first and join the second sleeve to the body in the same manner.

fINISHING

COLLAR

With A, shorter cir needle, and RS facing, k16 (17, 17, 19, 20) held right front neck sts, pick up and knit 5 sts along straight right neck selvedge, then 1 st in shoulder join, k42 (43, 44, 47, 50) held back neck sts, pick up and knit 1 st in shoulder join, then 5 sts along straight left neck selvedge, then k16 (17, 17, 19, 20) held left front neck sts—86 (89, 90, 97, 102) sts total. Work 7 rows in St st, beg and ending with a WS row. Purl 1 RS row for turning ridge. Work 7 rows in St st for facing, beg and ending with a WS row. BO all sts loosely. Fold facing to WS along turning ridge and with yarn threaded on a tapestry needle, sew BO edge in place along WS of pick-up row.

FRONT BANDS

With A and dpn, CO 12 sts. Work in twisted rib in rows until piece reaches from CO edge of lower body to turning ridge of collar when slightly stretched; about 18¼ (19¼, 20, 20½, 21½)" (46.5 [49, 51, 52, 54.5] cm). BO all sts. With A threaded on a tapestry needle, sew band to right front, easing to fit, and sewing through both layers of collar. Work a second twisted rib band and attach to left front in the same manner. Lay cardigan flat with fronts facing you. Mark positions for 7 clasps on each band, the highest centered on the collar, the lowest ¼" (6 mm) up from CO edge, and the rem 5 evenly spaced in between. Check the alignment of the clasp positions to make sure that the patterns will match across the front when the clasps are fastened. Sew clasps in place with A threaded on a tapestry needle.

Weave in loose ends. Press lightly on the WS with a warm iron over a damp cloth.

INGER SKI
CAP AND GLOVES

CAP

FINISHED SIZE

About 20" (51 cm) head circumference; will stretch to fit about 24" (61 cm).

YARN

Sportweight (#2 Super Fine).
Shown here: Dale of Norway Heilo (100% wool; 109/50 g): #4018 red (A), 3 balls; #0020 cream (B), 1 ball; #5813 light blue (C) and #5943 medium blue (D), small amounts of each.

NEEDLES

Size 3 mm (no exact U.S. equivalent; between U.S. size 2 and 3): set of 5 double-pointed (dpn). Adjust needle size if necessary to obtain the correct gauge.

NOTIONS

Marker (m); tapestry needle; piece of cardboard about 5" (12.5 cm) wide or CD jewel case for making tassel.

GAUGE

24 sts and 30 rounds = 4" (10 cm) in solid-color and "lice" pattern stockinette, worked in rounds; 32 rounds of Snowflake chart measure 4½" (11.5 cm) high.

Long knitted caps finished off with tassels have been worn in Norway for centuries. Although usually knitted in just two colors, caps for special occasions also include red, yellow, green, and blue and are densely patterned with initials and dates knitted into the design. The coordinating gloves were inspired by Norwegian handicrafts and the wonderful folk patterns of Selbu knitwear.

Both knitted in Dale of Norway's pure wool Heilo yarn, the cap features a traditional lice-stitch pattern and eight-point star and small amounts of duplicate stitch for extra color. Following tradition, the decorative tassel includes all the colors knitted in the hat. The gloves are worked on five needles and have a traditional Norwegian thumb gusset. Simple embroidery stitches add texture and color to the traditional motifs.

SNOWFLAKE

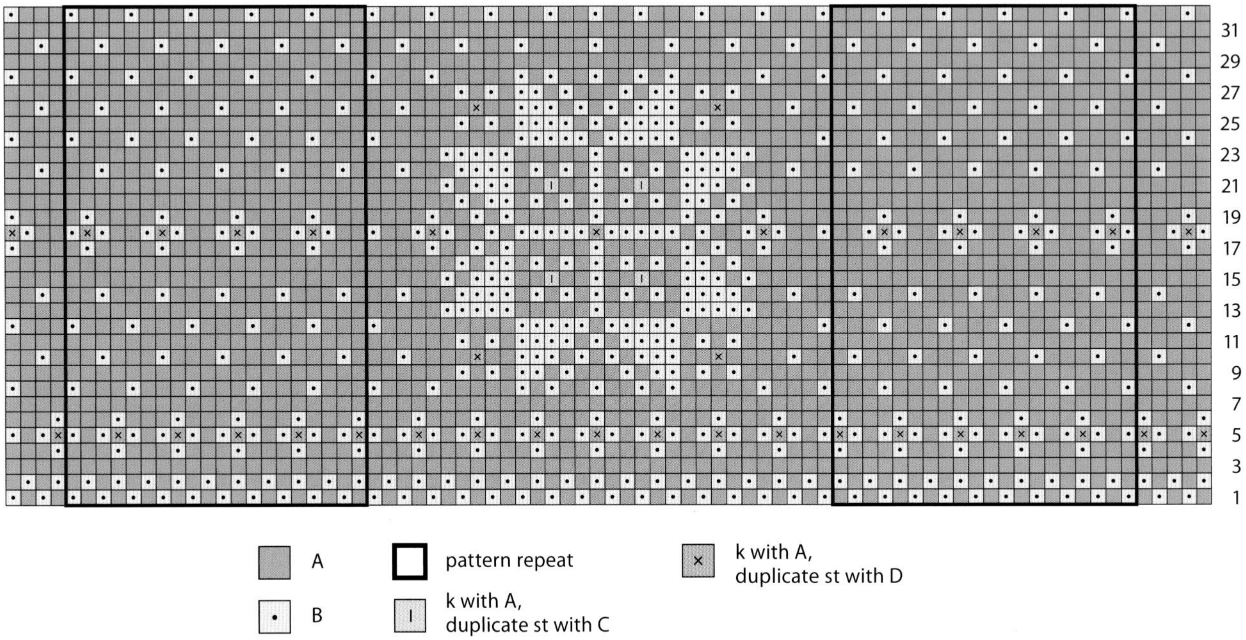

31
29
27
25
23
21
19
17
15
13
11
9
7
5
3
1
A
B
pattern repeat
k with A, duplicate st with C
k with A, duplicate st with D

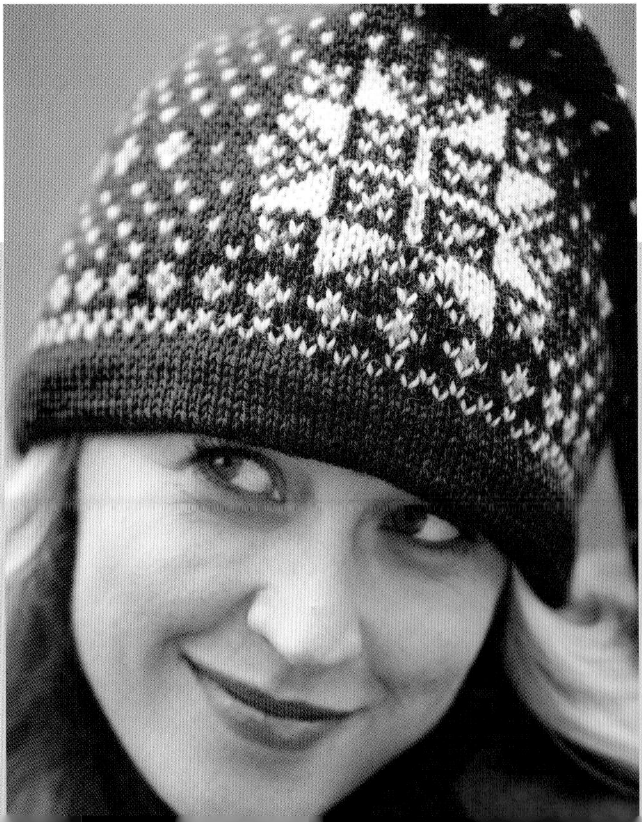

CAP

With A, CO 120 sts. Arrange the sts evenly on 4 dpn—30 sts each needle. Place marker (pm) and join for working rnds, being careful not to twist sts. Knit 18 rnds.

Next rnd: Establish patt from Rnd 1 of Snowflake chart as foll: Work 5 sts before first pattern repeat box once, work first 20-st repeat 2 times, work center 31 sts once, work second 20-st repeat 2 times, work 4 sts after second pattern repeat box once.

Cont in patt as established, work Rnds 2–32 of Snowflake chart—piece measures about 7" (18 cm) from CO.

SHAPE TOP

Rnd 1: With A, knit.

Rnd 2: (dec rnd) With A, *knit to last 2 sts on needle, ssk; rep from * 3 more times—1 st dec'd on each needle; 116 sts rem.

Rnd 3: With A, knit.

Rnd 4: ("lice" rnd) K1 A, *k1 B, k2 A; rep from * to last st, k1 B.

Rnd 5: With A, knit.

Rnd 6: With A, rep Rnd 2—4 sts dec'd; 112 sts rem.

Rnds 7–9: With A, knit.

Rnd 10: With A, rep Rnd 2—4 sts dec'd; 108 sts rem.

Rnd 11: With A, knit.

Rnd 12: (lice rnd) *K1 B, k2 A; rep from *.

Rnds 13–19: Rep Rnds 5–11—8 sts dec'd; 100 sts rem.

Rnd 20: (lice rnd) *K2 A, k1 B; rep from * to last st, k1 A.

Rnds 21–27: Rep Rnds 5–11—8 sts dec'd.

Rnd 28: (lice rnd) Rep Rnd 4.

Rnds 29–35: Rep Rnds 5–11—8 sts dec'd.

Rnd 36: (lice rnd) Rep Rnd 12.

Rnds 37–43: Rep Rnds 5–11—8 sts dec'd.

Rnd 44: (lice rnd) Rep Rnd 20.

Rnds 45–92: Rep Rnds 21–44 two times—28 sts rem.

Rnd 93: With A, knit.

Rnd 94: Rep Rnd 2—24 sts rem.

Rnds 95 and 96: With A, knit—piece measures 19¾" (50 cm) from CO.

Break yarn, leaving a 12" (30.5 cm) tail. Thread tail through rem sts, pull tight to close hole, and fasten off to WS.

FINISHING

Fold first 18 St st rnds in half for a 9-rnd hem, and, with A threaded on a tapestry needle, sew hem in place invisibly on WS. Weave in loose ends. With C and D, work duplicate stitches (see Glossary) as indicated on chart. With WS facing, press lightly with a cool iron over a damp cloth.

TASSEL

Holding all 4 colors tog, wrap the yarns around the cardboard or jewel case the desired number of times for tassel (see Glossary; the more wraps, the fatter the tassel). Attach tassel to point at top of hat.

GLOVES

FINISHED SIZE

About 8" (20.5 cm) hand circumference. To fit a woman's medium to large hand.

YARN

Sportweight (#2 Fine).
Shown here: Dale of Norway Heilo (100% wool; 109/50 g): #4018 red (A), 2 balls; #0020 cream (B), 1 ball; #2427 gold (C), #5943 medium blue (D), #5813 light blue (E), small amounts of each.

NEEDLES

Hand and fingers: Size 3 mm (no exact U.S. equivalent; between size U.S. 2 and 3): set of 5 double-pointed (dpn). *Fingertips:* Size U.S. 1 (2.5 mm): set of 4 or 5 dpn. Adjust needle size if necessary to obtain the correct gauge.

NOTIONS

Markers (m); smooth, contrasting waste yarn for stitch holders; tapestry needle.

GAUGE

26 stitches and 26 rounds = 4" (10 cm) in charted color patterns, worked in rounds on larger needles; 26 stitches and 32 rounds = 4" (10 cm) in solid-color stockinette, worked in rounds on larger needles.

LEFT GLOVE

CUFF

With A and larger needles, CO 44 sts. Arrange sts evenly onto 4 needles—11 sts each needle. Place marker (pm) and join for working in rnds, being careful not to twist sts; rnd begins at little finger side of hand. Work in p1, k3 rib for 25 rnds in stripes as foll: 7 rnds A, 2 rnds B, 2 rnds A, 1 rnd B, 1 rnd A, 1 rnd B, 2 rnds A, 2 rnds B, 7 rnds A—piece measures 3½" (9 cm) from CO.

HAND

Rearrange sts on 3 dpn so there are 11 sts on Needle 1, 10 sts on Needle 2, and 23 sts on Needle 3 (for the back of hand).

Next rnd: Beg and ending where indicated for left glove, establish patt from Rnd 1 of Hand chart by work 2-st patt rep box 9 times, then work next 26 sts.

Cont in patt from chart, work Rnds 2–5.

Next rnd: (Rnd 6 of chart) Keeping in patt, work 18 sts, pm, M1 (see Glossary) with A for start of thumb gusset, pm work in patt to end—1 st between gusset m.

Work Rnds 7–18 of chart—13 sts between gusset m; 57 sts total.

Next rnd: (Rnd 19 of chart) Keeping in patt, work 18 sts, remove gusset m and place the 13 gusset sts onto waste yarn to work later for thumb, use the backward-loop method (see Glossary) to CO 8 sts over thumb gap, alternating colors as shown, work to end in patt—52 hand sts.

Work until Rnd 28 of Hand chart is complete. Place sts on waste yarn. Work embroidery (see Glossary for embroidery stitches) as

HAND

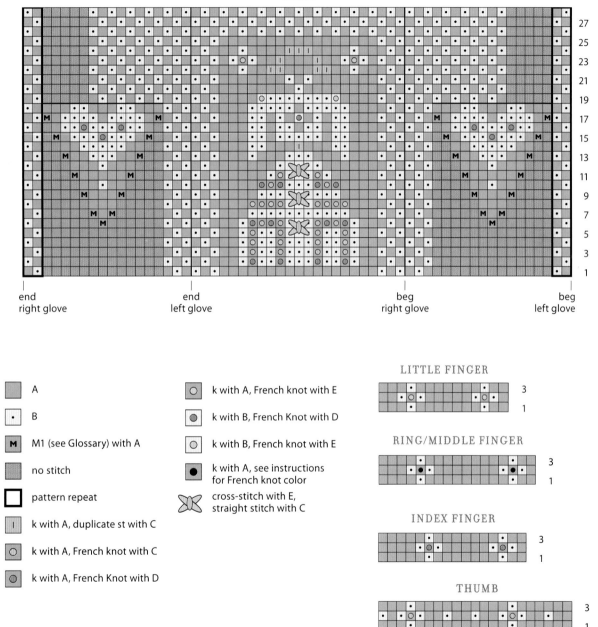

end right glove

end left glove

beg right glove

beg left glove

A

B

M M1 (see Glossary) with A

no stitch

pattern repeat

I k with A, duplicate st with C

○ k with A, French knot with C

◉ k with A, French Knot with D

○ k with A, French knot with E

◉ k with B, French Knot with D

○ k with B, French knot with E

● k with A, see instructions for French knot color

✕ cross-stitch with E, straight stitch with C

LITTLE FINGER

3

1

RING/MIDDLE FINGER

3

1

INDEX FINGER

3

1

THUMB

3

1

indicated on chart as foll: With gold, work duplicate stitches. Work three cross-stitches with light blue, then work a small vertical straight stitch with gold in the center of each cross-stitch. Work French knots with light blue, medium blue, and gold.

LITTLE FINGER

With palm side of glove facing, A, and beg at side of hand at original beg-of-rnd, knit the first 5 palm sts, use the backward-loop method (see Glossary) to CO 2 sts, then knit the last 7 back-of-hand sts (last 7 sts of original rnd)—14 sts total. Arrange sts as evenly as possible onto 3 dpn and join for working in rnds. Knit 2 rnds. Work Rnds 1–3 of Little Finger chart. With A, knit 1 rnd. With light blue, embroider French knots as shown. With A, knit 12 more rnds, or until finger reaches middle of fingernail.

SHAPE TIP

Change to smaller dpn and work as foll:
Rnd 1: *K1, ssk; rep from * to last 2 sts, k2—10 sts rem.
Rnd 2: [Ssk] 5 times—5 sts rem.
Cut yarn, thread tail through rem sts, pull tight to close the hole, and fasten off on the WS.

RING FINGER

With palm side of glove facing and A, knit the next 7 palm sts, use the backward-loop method to CO 2 sts, knit the last 6 back-of-hand sts, pick up and knit 2 sts at base of sts CO for little finger—17 sts total. Arrange sts as evenly as possible onto 3 dpn and join for working in rnds. Knit 2 rnds. Work Rnds 1–3 of Ring/Middle Finger chart. With A, knit 1 rnd. With medium

blue, embroider French knots as shown. With A, knit 15 more rnds, or until finger reaches middle of fingernail. Shape the tip as for little finger—12 sts rem after Rnd 1; 6 sts rem after Rnd 2. Close tip as for little finger.

MIDDLE FINGER

With palm side of glove facing and A, knit the next 7 palm sts, use the backward-loop method to CO 2 sts, knit the last 6 back-of-hand sts, pick up and knit 2 sts at base of sts CO for ring finger—17 sts total. Arrange sts as evenly as possible onto 3 dpn and join for working in rnds. Knit 2 rnds. Work Rnds 1–3 of Ring/Middle Finger chart. With A, knit 1 rnd. With light blue, embroider French knots as shown. With A, knit 16 more rnds, or until finger reaches middle of fingernail. Shape the tip as for little finger—12 sts rem after Rnd 1; 6 sts rem after Rnd 2. Close tip as for little finger.

INDEX FINGER

With palm side of glove facing and A, knit the rem 14 sts, pick up and knit 2 sts at base of sts CO for middle finger—16 sts total. Arrange sts as evenly as possible onto 3 dpn and join for working in rnds. Knit 2 rnds. Work Rnds 1–3 of Index Finger chart. With A, knit 1 rnd. With medium blue, embroider French knots as shown. With A, knit 14 more rnds, or until finger reaches middle of fingernail.

SHAPE TIP

Change to smaller dpn and work as foll:
Rnd 1: K1,*ssk, k1; rep from *—11 sts rem.
Rnd 2: [Ssk] 5 times, k1—6 sts rem.
Close tip as for little finger.

THUMB

Return 13 held thumb sts to dpn. With A, k13 thumb sts, then pick up and knit 8 sts from base of sts CO over thumb gap for hand—21 sts total. Arrange sts evenly on 3 dpn and join for working in rnds. Knit 2 rnds. Work Rnds 1–3 of Thumb chart. With A, knit 1 rnd. With gold, embroider French knots as shown.

Next rnd: Work ssk at beg of Needle 1, at the end of Needle 2, and in the center of Needle 3—18 sts rem.

Knit 11 rnds, or until finger reaches middle of fingernail.

SHAPE TIP

Change to smaller dpn and work as foll:

Rnd 1: *K1, ssk; rep from *—12 sts rem.

Rnd 2: [Ssk] 6 times—6 sts rem.

Close tip as for little finger.

RIGHT GLOVE

CUFF

Work as for left glove—44 sts; piece measures 3½" (9 cm) from CO; rnd begins at little finger side of hand.

HAND

Rearrange sts on 3 dpn so there are 23 sts on Needle 1 (for the back of hand), 10 sts on Needle 2, and 11 sts on Needle 3.

Next rnd: Beg and ending where indicated for right glove, establish patt from Rnd 1 of Hand chart by working 26 sts, then rep 2-st patt rep box 9 times.

Cont in patt from chart, work Rnds 2–5.

Next rnd: (Rnd 6 of chart) Keeping in patt, work 26 sts, pm, M1 with A for start of thumb gusset, pm, work in patt to end—1 st between gusset m. Work Rnds 7–18 of chart—13 sts between gusset m; 57 sts total.

Next rnd: (Rnd 19 of chart) Keeping in patt, work 26 sts, remove gusset m and place the 13 gusset sts onto waste yarn, use the backward-loop method to CO 8 sts over thumb gap, alternating colors as shown, work to end in patt—52 hand sts.

Work until Rnd 28 of Hand chart is complete. Place sts on waste yarn to work later for thumb. Work embroidery as for left glove.

FINGERS AND THUMB

Holding glove with back-of-hand facing as you start each finger, work little, ring, middle, and index fingers (in that order) as for left glove. Work thumb as for left glove.

FINISHING

Weave in loose ends, using yarn tails to close up any holes at base of fingers. Press lightly with a cool iron over a damp cloth.

Liv Patterned

SOCKS

FINISHED SIZE

About 9¼" (23.5 cm) foot circumference, 11½" (29 cm) leg length from CO to end of heel flap, and 9½" (24 cm) foot length from back of heel to tip of toe. To fit women's U.S. shoe sizes 7–9 with a loose, slipper-like fit.

YARN

Sportweight (#2 Fine).
Shown here: Dale of Norway Heilo (100% wool; 109 yd/50 g): #5943 medium blue (A) and #0020 cream (B), 2 balls each; #5813 light blue (C), 1 ball; #4018 red (D) and #2427 gold (E), small amounts of each.

NEEDLES

Size 3 mm (no exact U.S. equivalent; between U.S. sizes 2 and 3): set of 5 double-pointed (dpn). Adjust needle size if necessary to obtain the correct gauge.

NOTIONS

Marker (m); waste yarn holder; tapestry needle.

GAUGE

26 stitches and 26 rounds = 4" (10 cm) in charted color pattern, worked in rounds.

Just as there has always been the need to protect hands from the bitter cold Norwegian winters, so there has been a need to protect the feet. During the second half of the eighteenth century there was a tradition in Norway for knitting *strømpe*— long, elaborately patterned socks with textured, patterned, or openwork cuffs. As with the original *strømpe*, these Liv socks are knitted on five needles and have several different age-old folk designs— dancing figures, eight-leaf roses, lice stitch, a decorative cuff, and a star toe.

Knitted in Dale of Norway's pure wool Heilo yarn, these socks are not only lovely to look at, but are truly warm and comfortable.

NOTES

· The socks are worked from the cuff down, and the chart is oriented in the same direction as the knitting. When the socks are worn, the dancers in the chart will appear right-side up, as shown in the photographs.

· In the gusset shaping, the ssk decrease is deliberately used on both sides of the gusset. If you would prefer mirror-image decreases, use k2tog at the end of Needle 1 and ssk at the beginning of Needle 3.

· For a longer foot, knit extra plain rounds with color C before beginning the toe decreases. Every 3 additional rounds will add about ½" (1.3 cm) to the foot length.

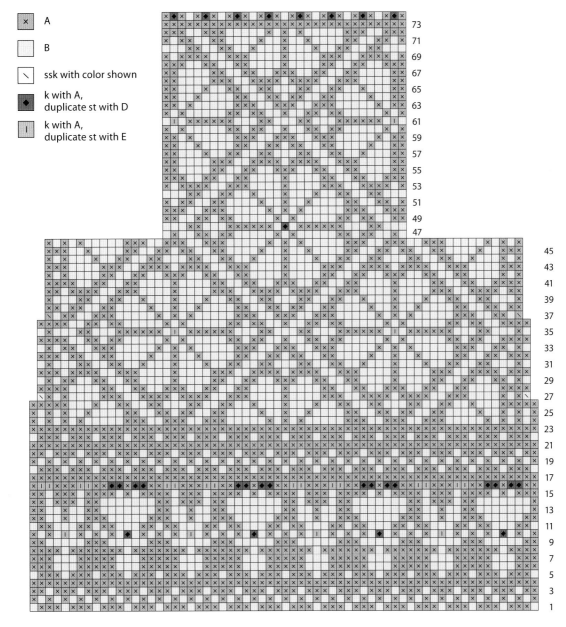

Legend:

- × | A
- □ | B
- ╲ | ssk with color shown
- ◆ | k with A, duplicate st with D
- ⌶ | k with A, duplicate st with E

SOCK

CUFF

With A, CO 65 sts. Arrange sts as evenly as possible on 3 dpn, place marker (pm), and join for working in rnds, being careful not to twist sts; rnd begins at center back leg. Work chevron patt as foll:

Rnd 1: With A, *k1, yo, k4, k2tog, ssk, k4, yo; rep from *.

Rnd 2: With A, knit.

Rnds 3–10: Rep Rnds 1 and 2 four more times.

Rnds 11 and 12: With B, rep Rnds 1 and 2.

Rnds 13 and 14: With A, rep Rnds 1 and 2.

Rnds 15 and 16: With B, rep Rnds 1 and 2.

Rnds 17–20: With A, rep Rnds 1 and 2 once, then knit 2 rnds—piece measures 2½" (6.5 cm) from CO at deepest point of chevron.

LEG

Work Rnds 1–46 of Dancers and Snowflakes chart (see Notes), dec 1 st at each end of rnd as shown in Rnds 27 and 37—61 sts rem; piece measures 9½" (24 cm) from CO. Break yarns.

HEEL

Place the 15 sts on each side of end-of-rnd m on a single needle for heel, removing the m as you come to it—30 sts on heel needle. Place rem 31 sts on waste yarn holder or divide on 2 needles to work later for instep.

HEEL FLAP

Join C to beg of 30 heel sts with RS facing and knit 1 row. *Note:* Slip-stitches as if to purl with yarn in back on RS rows and with yarn in front on WS rows.

Row 1: (WS) Sl 1, purl to end.

Row 2: (RS) *Sl 1, k1; rep from * to end.

Rep Rows 1 and 2 nine times, then work WS Row 1 once more—22 rows total; flap measures about 2" (5 cm).

TURN HEEL

Work short-rows as foll:

Row 1: (RS) K17, ssk, k1, turn work.

Row 2: (WS) Sl 1, p5, p2tog, p1, turn.

Row 3: Sl 1, k6, ssk, k1, turn.

Row 4: Sl 1, p7, p2tog, p1, turn.

Row 5: Sl 1, k8, ssk, k1, turn.

Row 6: Sl 1, p9, p2tog, p1, turn.

Row 7: Sl 1, k10, ssk, k1, turn.

Row 8: Sl 1, p11, p2tog, p1, turn.

Row 9: Sl 1, k12, ssk, k1, turn.

Row 10: Sl 1, p13, p2tog, p1, turn.

Row 11: Sl 1, k14, ssk, k1, turn.

Row 12: Sl 1, p15, p2tog, p1, turn—18 heel sts rem.

SHAPE GUSSET

Break off C. Arrange the heel sts on 2 needles—9 sts each needle. Rejoin A and B with RS facing to start of second heel needle; rnd begins at center of heel.

Pick-up rnd: With Needle 1, knit 9 heel sts alternating 1 st each of A and B, beg and ending with k1 A, then pick up and knit 11 sts along selvedge of heel flap in alternating colors as established, ending with k1 B; with Needle 2, work Rnd 47 of chart across 31 instep sts; with Needle 3, pick up and knit 11 sts along other

selvedge of heel flap using alternating colors, beg and ending with k1 B, then knit rem 9 heel sts, alternating colors and ending with k1 A—71 sts total; 20 heel and gusset sts each on Needle 1 and Needle 3; 31 instep sts on Needle 2.

Rnd 1: On Needle 1, knit each st with its opposite color to last 3 sts, ssk in color to maintain alternation (see Notes), k1 B (always work this st with B); on Needle 2, work next chart rnd; on Needle 3, k1 B (always work this st with B), ssk in color to maintain alternation, then knit each st with its opposite color to end—2 sts dec'd.

Rnd 2: On Needle 1, knit each st with its opposite color to last st, k1 B; on Needle 2, work next chart rnd; on Needle 3, k1 B, knit each st with its opposite color to end.

Rep Rnds 1 and 2 three more times, then rep Rnd 1 once more—61 sts rem; 15 sole sts each on Needle 1 and Needle 3; 31 instep sts on Needle 2.

FOOT

Work until Rnd 72 of chart on Needle 2 is complete, cont to work k1 B at end of Needle 1 and beg of Needle 3, and knitting each sole st with its opposite color.

Next rnd: (Rnd 73 of chart) Knit all sts with A.

Next rnd: (Rnd 74 of chart) On Needles 1 and 3, knit each st with same color used in Rnd 72; on Needle 2, work Rnd 74 of chart—foot measures about 6½" (16.5 cm) long from center back heel (see Notes for adjusting length). Break yarns.

SHAPE TOE

Join C, knit to last 2 sts of rnd, ssk—60 sts rem. Redistribute sts evenly on 4 dpn—15 sts each needle.

Rnds 1–3: Knit.

Rnd 4: On each needle, knit to last 2 sts, k2tog—4 sts dec'd; 56 sts rem.

Rnds 5 and 6: Knit.

Rnd 7: Rep Rnd 4—52 sts rem.

Rnds 8 and 9: Knit.

Rnd 10: Rep Rnd 4—48 sts rem.

Rnd 11: Knit.

Rnds 12–19: Rep Rnds 10 and 11 four more times—32 sts rem.

Rnds 20–25: Rep Rnd 4 (dec every rnd) 6 times—8 sts rem; solid-color St st toe measures about 3" (7.5 cm) from end of chart patt.

Break yarn, leaving a 10" (25.5 cm) tail. Thread the tail through rem sts, pull tight to close the hole, and fasten off on the WS.

fINISHING

Weave in loose ends. With D and E, work duplicate stitches (see Glossary) as indicated on chart. Press lightly with a cool iron over a damp cloth.

SWEDEN

Handknitting is one of the most treasured and well known of all the Swedish handicrafts. It has been popular in Sweden since the late 1500s, and the introduction of knitting to rural Sweden can be traced back to the Halland region in about 1650. Magna Brita Cracaus, a wealthy Dutch woman who had learned to knit in Holland, taught all her servants to knit stockings and shirts with wool yarn. The technique became popular and, before long, knitted garments became an important means of trade.

Although conventional knitting was practiced, the vast majority of early Swedish knitting, especially in the Northern areas, was *tvåändsstickat*—"two-ended," or twined knitting. This technique, in which both ends of the same ball of yarn are used and the two ends are twisted around each other after each stitch, produces a uniform fabric of double thickness that is smooth, firm, warm, and hard wearing. It is perfectly suited for mittens and socks, and being less elastic than conventional knitting, twined knitting forms an ideal base for embroidery. Extra time and effort was taken to knit for festive and special occasions, and mittens were heavily embroidered with various stylized flowers, leaves, and hearts and included colorful tufted borders and edgings. Crook stitches (distinctive raised patterning effects achieved only with twined knitting) were also used as decoration.

The patterns that started to emerge on all rural knitwear—stars, diamonds, and hearts—were common to, and certainly inspired by, embroidery and weaving. Regional specialties of color and pattern evolved, such as the red, green, black, and white women's jackets from Delsbo Halsingland, the white wool mittens with red and white patterned borders from Dalarna, and the predominantly white fisherman's sweaters with red and blue bands of patterning from Uppland.

By the middle of the 1800s, magazines and pattern books made knitting patterns highly accessible and knitting styles become more homogenized across the country. This, combined with the introduction of cheaper industrially machine-made knitwear, caused a decline in the need for traditional folk textiles made in the traditional way. Toward the end of the 1800s, however, there was a resurgence of interest in handicrafts and folk art of rural Sweden. The Nordiska Museet was founded in 1873 and the Skansen open air museum in 1891. In 1874, the progressive Handarbetets Vänner was founded and its vision, *skonhet for alla*—beauty for all—encouraged simplicity and comfort in the home with the use of affordable bright traditional textiles. Early advocates of this movement were artists Karin and Carl Larsson and Lilli Zickerman, who subsequently founded the Swedish Handicraft Association in 1899.

Lilli Zickerman set up many regional craft organizations across Sweden, and her vision for accessible high-quality, locally made handicrafts inspired future generations. In 1939, Emma Jacobsson set up Bohus Stickning to promote local knitwear traditions. This subsequently became an internationally renowned knitwear company synonymous with beautifully colored and patterned high-quality knitwear.

A visit to the Nordiska Museet in Stockholm, with its fantastic tapestries and textiles, fueled my imagination and inspired me to design the following projects. Enthused by learning the ancient folk craft of twined knitting, I created designs using Ullcentrum's beautiful, pure Swedish wool that continue the old traditions while remaining comfortable, useful, and contemporary.

OLA PLACKET
PULLOVER

FINISHED SIZE

35¾ (39, 43, 47, 51)" (91 [99, 109, 119.5, 129.5] cm) bust circumference.
Sweater shown measures 47" (119.5 cm).

YARN

Sportweight (#2 Fine).
Shown here: Ullcentrum Oland 2-Thread Wool Yarn (100% wool; 328 yd [300 m]/100 g): cream (A), 4 (5, 5, 5, 6) skeins; red (B), 1 skein; and petrol (C), small amount.

NEEDLES

Size 3 mm (no exact U.S. equivalent; between U.S. sizes 2 and 3): 16" and 32" (40 and 80 cm) circular (cir), and set of 4 double-pointed (dpn). Adjust needle size if necessary to obtain the correct gauge.

NOTIONS

Marker (m); stitch holders; tapestry needle.

GAUGE

24 stitches and 35 rounds/rows = 4" (10 cm) in stockinette stitch.

In the Nordiska Museet in Stockholm, there are some beautiful examples of simple white linen work shirts and shifts that have embroidered details of hearts, stylized flowers, and birds at the neckline and on the sleeves. The shortish and loose-fitting Ola sweater is a knitted version of those embroidered shirts. Using pure two-strand white Swedish wool, both the sleeves and the main body are knitted in the round, then embellished with simple cross-stitches and French knots. The three-quarter-length sleeves begin with a lovely red and white twined knitted cast-on. This sweater is ideal for layering.

NOTES

· The lower body and lower sleeves are worked in the round to the start of the armholes. The upper back, upper front, and sleeve caps are worked separately, back and forth in rows.

· The body is worked entirely in stockinette with A, then the neckline embroidery is worked in duplicate stitch and French knots during finishing.

· Although the lower part of the sleeve is worked in the round, the sleeve is shown opened out flat on the schematic because the cap is worked back and forth in rows.

· For a longer lower body, work more rounds in stockinette between the last decrease round and where the piece divides for front and back. For longer sleeves, work more rounds after the last increase round and before starting the cap shaping. Every 9 rounds added will lengthen the piece by about 1" (2.5 cm).

STITCH GUIDE

TWINED PURLING

*With both strands in front, insert right needle into next st on left needle as if to purl, bring the strand farthest from the tip of the right needle under the other strand, and use it to purl the stitch; rep from * alternating the 2 strands and bringing each strand under the one used before.

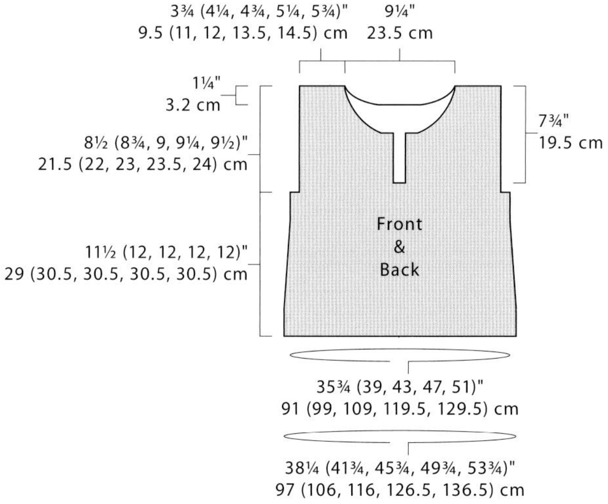
3¾ (4¼, 4¾, 5¼, 5¾)"
9.5 (11, 12, 13.5, 14.5) cm
9¼"
23.5 cm
1¼"
3.2 cm
8½ (8¾, 9, 9¼, 9½)"
21.5 (22, 23, 23.5, 24) cm
7¾"
19.5 cm
11½ (12, 12, 12, 12)"
29 (30.5, 30.5, 30.5, 30.5) cm
Front
&
Back
35¾ (39, 43, 47, 51)"
91 (99, 109, 119.5, 129.5) cm
38¼ (41¾, 45¾, 49¾, 53¾)"
97 (106, 116, 126.5, 136.5) cm

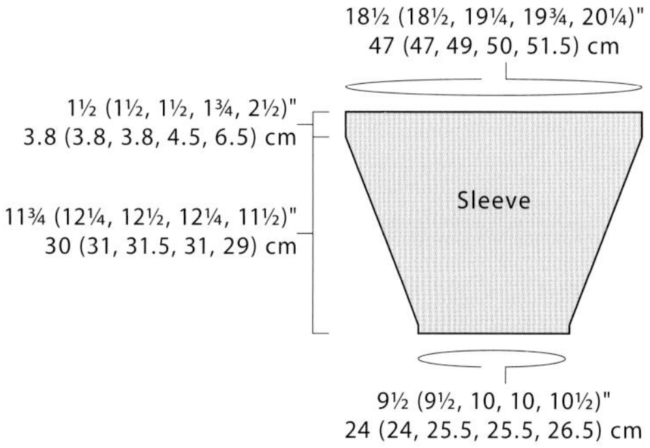
18½ (18½, 19¼, 19¾, 20¼)"
47 (47, 49, 50, 51.5) cm
1½ (1½, 1½, 1¾, 2½)"
3.8 (3.8, 3.8, 4.5, 6.5) cm
11¾ (12¼, 12½, 12¼, 11½)"
30 (31, 31.5, 31, 29) cm
Sleeve
9½ (9½, 10, 10, 10½)"
24 (24, 25.5, 25.5, 26.5) cm

TWINED CAST-ON
WITH DOUBLE BEAD

Leaving long tails for braiding later, make a slipknot
with 2 strands of A and 1 strand of B, and place the
slipknot on the needle; the slipknot does not count as
a CO st. Hold B in your left hand and the needle and
2 strands of A in your right hand **(Figure 1)**. Loop B
around the left thumb. Slip the needle tip underneath
both strands of the loop, between the loop and the web
of your thumb (and not into the loop itself yet). Next,
insert the right needle tip down into the thumb loop
from top to bottom **(Figure 2)** and rotate the needle so
its tip is pointing upward again—the thumb loop now
forms a figure-eight, with the thumb and needle in
separate compartments of the eight **(Figure 3)**. Wrap
one strand of A around the needle as if to knit.

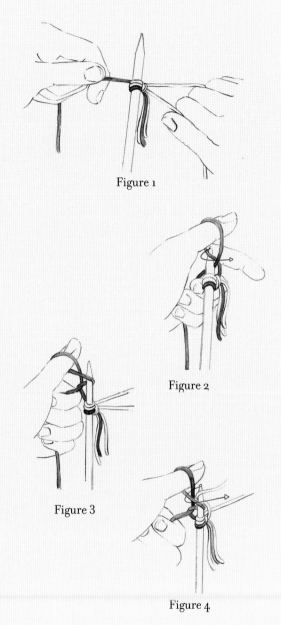

Figure 1

Figure 2

Figure 3

Figure 4

Insert the needle tip up into the thumb loop from
bottom to top **(Figure 4**; this will undo the twist of the
figure-eight**)**, drop the B loop from the left thumb,
and tighten the new st.*Loop B around left thumb
again, slip needle tip underneath both strands of the
loop, then insert it down into the thumb loop from
top to bottom. Rotate the needle so its tip is pointing upward again, bring the strand of A farthest from
the needle tip over the previous strand of A used,
and wrap it around the needle as if to knit. Insert the
needle tip up into the thumb loop from bottom to top,
drop the B loop from the left thumb, and tighten the
new st; rep from * until the required number of sts
are CO, alternating strands of A and bringing each
strand over the one used before. Break off B. Drop the
slipknot from the needle before joining in the rnd but
do not untie it yet.

FRONT EMBROIDERY

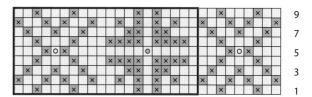

k with A on all rnds and RS rows;
p with A on WS rows

× on sleeve chart,
k on RS, p on WS with B;
on front embroidery diagram,
work St st with A, duplicate st with B

○ k with A,
French knot with A

◉ k with A,
French knot with C

pattern repeat

SLEEVE

BODY

With A and longer cir needle, CO 230 (250, 274, 298, 322) sts. Place marker (pm) and join for working in rnds; rnd begins at left side, at start of front sts. Knit 15 rnds. Purl 1 rnd for hem turning ridge. Knit 19 rnds, pm for right side after first 115 (125, 137, 149, 161) sts in last rnd—piece measures 2¼" (5.5 cm) from turning ridge.

Dec rnd: K1, k2tog through back loops (tbl), knit to 3 sts before right side m, k2tog, k1, slip marker (sl m), k1, k2tog tbl, knit to last 3 sts, k2tog, k1—4 sts dec'd; 2 sts each from front and back.

*Knit 19 rnds even, then rep dec rnd; rep from * 2 more times—214 (234, 258, 282, 306) sts rem; 107 (117, 129, 141, 153) sts each for front and back. Work even in St st until piece measures 11½ (12, 12, 12, 12)" (29 [30.5, 30.5, 30.5, 30.5] cm) from CO or desired length (see Notes).

FRONT

Begin working front and back separately, back and forth in rows, as foll:

Next row: (RS) BO 3 (5, 8, 11, 15) sts for left front armhole, knit until there are 104 (112, 121, 130, 138) front sts on needle after BO gap, place rem 107 (117, 129, 141, 153) sts on holder to work later for back.

Next row: (WS) BO 3 (5, 8, 11, 15) sts for right front armhole, purl to end—101 (107, 113, 119, 123) sts rem.

Work 2 (4, 6, 6, 8) rows even in St st, ending with a WS row.

SHAPE NECK

Next row: (RS) K45 (48, 51, 54, 56) join new
yarn, BO center 11 sts, knit to end—45 (48, 51,
54, 56) sts rem each side.

Working each side separately, work even in St st
for 35 rows, beg and ending with a WS row—front
neck opening measures about 4" (10 cm). At each
neck edge, BO 5 sts once—40 (43, 46, 49, 51) sts rem
each side. Dec 1 st at each neck edge every row 10
times, then every other row 4 times, then every
4th row 3 times—23 (26, 29, 32, 34) sts rem each
side. Work even in St st if necessary until armholes
measure 8½ (8¾, 9, 9¼, 9½)" (21.5 [22, 23,
23.5, 24] cm). Place sts on separate holders.

BACK

Return 107 (117, 129, 141, 153) held back sts to
longer cir needle and rejoin yarn with RS facing.
Working in St st, BO 3 (5, 8, 11, 15) st at beg of
next 2 rows—101 (107, 113, 119, 123) sts rem.
Work even in St st until armholes measure 7¼
(7½, 7¾, 8, 8¼)" (18.5 [19, 19.5, 20.5, 21] cm),
ending with a WS row.

SHAPE NECK

Next row: (RS) K40 (43, 46, 49, 51), place center
21 sts on holder, join new yarn, knit to end—
40 (43, 46, 49, 51) sts rem each side.

Working each side separately, at each neck edge
BO 5 sts 3 times, then BO 1 st 2 times—23 (26,
29, 32, 34) sts rem each side. Work even in St st
if necessary until armholes measure 8½ (8¾, 9,
9¼, 9½)" (21.5 [22, 23, 23.5, 24] cm). Place sts
on separate holders.

SLEEVES

With dpn and using the twined method with a double bead (see page 116), CO 57 (57, 61, 61, 65) sts. Pm and join for working in rnds, being careful not to twist sts. With A, work 2 rnds of twined purling (see Stitch Guide)—piece measures about ¼" (6 mm). *Note:* The strands will twist around each other as you work; to undo the twist, periodically allow the sleeve to dangle and twirl freely in midair. Break off one strand of A and cont in St st with A using a single strand. Knit 1 rnd.

Inc rnd: K1, M1 (see Glossary), knit to last st, M1, k1—2 sts inc'd.

Cont in St st, rep the inc rnd every 2nd rnd 9 (9, 9, 11, 10) times, then every 4th rnd 10 times, then every 5th rnd 7 times, changing to shorter cir needle when there are too many sts to fit on dpns—111 (111, 115, 119, 121) sts.

Work even in St st until piece measures 11¾ (12¼, 12½, 12¼, 11½)" (30 [31, 31.5, 31, 29] cm) or about 1½ (1½, 1½, 1¾, 2½)" (3.8 [3.8, 3.8, 4.5, 6.5] cm) less than desired length. *Note:* The larger sizes have taller sleeve caps, so their lower sleeves are shorter to prevent the cuff-to-cuff "wingspan" of the sweater from becoming too wide.

SHAPE CAP

Remove end-of-rnd m and change to working St st back and forth in rows. Beg and ending with a WS purl row, work 1 (1, 1, 3, 9) row(s) even in St st.

Next row: (RS) K1 (1, 3, 5, 6) with A, work Row 1 of Sleeve chart over center 109 sts, k1 (1, 3, 5, 6) with A. *Note:* For the three larger sizes, use B only within the chart area; do not strand B all the way to the selvedges.

Working St sts in A as established at each side, work Rows 2–9 of chart. With A, work 3 rows even in St st, beg and ending with a WS row—piece measures 13¼, (13¾, 14, 14, 14)" (33.5 [35, 35.5, 35.5, 35.5] cm) from CO. BO all sts.

fINISHINg

JOIN SHOULDERS

Place held right shoulder sts of front and back on separate cir needles and hold pieces tog with RS touching and WS facing outward. With A and one tip of longer needle or a single dpn, use the three-needle method (see Glossary) to join shoulder sts tog. Join left shoulder sts in the same manner.

NECKBAND

With A, shorter cir needle, RS facing, and beg at top right corner of neck opening, pick up and knit 32 sts along right front neck, 20 sts along right back neck, k21 held center back sts, pick up and knit 20 sts along left back neck, and 32 sts along left front neck—125 sts total. Work 3 rows in St st, beg and ending with a WS row. Purl 1 RS row for turning ridge. Work 3 rows in St st for facing. With RS facing, BO all sts knitwise. Fold facing to WS along turning ridge and, with yarn threaded on a tapestry needle, sew in place along WS of pick-up row, leaving short selvedges at end of neckband open for drawstring casing. Work a braided drawstring using two strands of A and one strand of B for about 44" (112 cm). Tie each end in an overhand knot and trim ends. Thread drawstring through neckband as shown.

EMBROIDERY

Work duplicate-stitch embroidery with B and French knots with A and C (see Glossary for embroidery stitches) around front neck opening as shown in Front Embroidery chart. Work French knots with A and C on sleeves as shown on Sleeve chart.

Weave in loose ends. Fold lower body hem to WS along turning ridge and with yarn threaded on a tapestry needle, sew invisibly in place on WS. Sew sleeves into armholes, easing to fit, then sew short sleeve seams at top of sections worked in rounds if necessary for your size.

Wash the sweater in warm soapy water and gently roll in a towel to squeeze out excess water. Pull gently into shape and leave to dry flat. Once dry press carefully on the WS with a warm iron over a damp cloth.

PIA LACEWEIGHT
PULLOVER

FINISHED SIZE

35 (38, 40¾, 43½, 46½, 49¼)" (89 [96.5, 103.5, 110.5, 118, 125] bust circumference.
Sweater shown measures 38" (96.5 cm).

YARN

Laceweight (#0 Lace).
Shown here: Ullcentrum Öland 1-Thread Wool Yarn (100% wool; 656 yd [600 m]/100 g): marbled gray, 3 (3, 3, 3, 4, 4) skeins.

NEEDLES

Size 3 mm (no exact U.S. equivalent; between U.S. sizes 2 and 3): 16" and 32" (40 and 80 cm) circular (cir) and set of 4 or 5 double-pointed (dpn). Adjust needle size if necessary to obtain the correct gauge.

NOTIONS

Marker (m); stitch holder; tapestry needle.

GAUGE

36 stitches and 56 rounds (3 pattern repeats wide and 2 pattern repeats high) measure 4¼" (11 cm) wide and 5¼" (13.5 cm) high in charted lace pattern, after blocking; 29 stitches and 40 rows/rounds = 4" (10 cm) in stockinette stitch, after blocking.

Swedish wool, with its long and glossy fibers, is usually of a very high quality, and Ullcentrum's pure wool 1-ply lace yarn is no exception. Sourced predominantly from the island of Öland, which sits just off the Swedish coast in the Baltic Sea, this yarn is gorgeously soft and light. Pia's sleeves and body are knitted in the round to the armholes. The marbled gray variegated natural tones of the yarn gives this light, easy-to-wear lacy sweater a distinctive Swedish look. Once completed, the sweater is washed in warm soapy water to create a slightly felted look and feel.

NOTES

- The lower body and lower sleeves are worked in the round to the base of the armholes. The upper back, upper front, and sleeve caps are worked separately, back and forth in rows.

- Although the lower part of the sleeve is worked in the round, the sleeve is drawn opened out flat on the schematic to show the shape of the cap.

- The lower body and sleeves contain the same number of lace pattern rounds for all sizes. To add length, work extra 28-round repeats of the pattern without any shaping at the beginning of each piece, then proceed to Round 1 of the instructions. Every 28-round repeat added will increase the length of the piece by about 2½" (6.5 cm). Plan on purchasing extra yarn if making a longer body or sleeves.

- The fine single-ply yarn used here has a tendency to bias and may need to be blocked firmly to reduce the amount of slant in the finished fabric.

BODY

With longer cir needle, CO 348 (372, 396, 420, 444, 468) sts. Place marker (pm) and join for working in rnds, being careful not to twist sts; rnd begins at left side at start of front sts. If making a longer body, see Notes.

Rnd 1: *K15, pm, work Rnd 1 of Lace chart (see page 126) over 145 (157, 169, 181, 193, 205) sts, pm, k14; rep from * once more.

Rnds 2–10: Working sts outside marked sections in St st, work 9 rnds even, ending with Rnd 10 of chart.

Rnd 11: (dec rnd) *Knit to 2 sts before m, k2tog, slip marker (sl m), cont lace patt as established to next m, sl m, ssk, knit to next m; rep from * once more—4 sts dec'd; 1 st at each end of each St st side panel.

Rnds 12–20: Cont in patts, work 9 rnds even, ending with Rnd 20 of chart.

Rnd 21: (dec rnd) Rep Rnd 11—340 (364, 388, 412, 436, 460) sts.

Rnds 22–28: Cont in patts, work 7 rnds even, ending with Rnd 28 of chart.

Rnds 29–56: Cont in patts, work Rnds 1–28 of chart and *at the same time* work decs as for Rnd 11 on Rnds 3, 13, and 23—328 (352, 376, 400, 424, 448) sts rem.

Rnds 57–84: Cont in patts, work Rnds 1–28 of chart and *at the same time* work decs as for Rnd 11 on Rnds 5, 15, and 25—316 (340, 364, 388, 412, 436) sts rem.

Rnds 85–112: Cont in patts, work Rnds 1–28 of chart and *at the same time* work decs as for Rnd 11 on Rnds 7, 17, and 27—304 (328, 352, 376, 400, 424) sts rem.

Rnds 113–140: Cont in patts, work Rnds 1–28 of chart and *at the same time* work decs as for Rnd 11 on Rnds 9 and 19, and end last rnd 2 (5, 7, 8, 9, 10) sts before end-of-rnd m—296 (320, 344, 368, 392, 416) sts rem; 2 lace panels with 145 (157, 169, 181, 193, 205) sts each; 2 St sts before first lace panel, 3 St sts between lace panels, 1 St st between second lace panel and end-of-rnd m; piece will measure 13" (33 cm) after blocking.

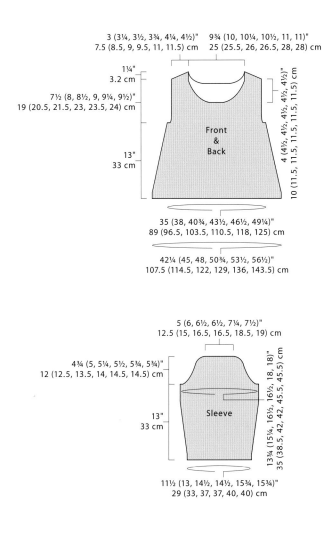

3 (3¼, 3½, 3¾, 4¼, 4½)"
7.5 (8.5, 9, 9.5, 11, 11.5) cm

9¾ (10, 10¼, 10½, 11, 11)"
25 (25.5, 26, 26.5, 28, 28) cm

1¼"
3.2 cm

7½ (8, 8½, 9, 9¼, 9½)"
19 (20.5, 21.5, 23, 23.5, 24) cm

4 (4½, 4½, 4½, 4½, 4½)"
10 (11.5, 11.5, 11.5, 11.5, 11.5) cm

Front & Back

13"
33 cm

35 (38, 40¾, 43½, 46½, 49¼)"
89 (96.5, 103.5, 110.5, 118, 125) cm

42¼ (45, 48, 50¾, 53½, 56½)"
107.5 (114.5, 122, 129, 136, 143.5) cm

5 (6, 6½, 6½, 7¼, 7½)"
12.5 (15, 16.5, 16.5, 18.5, 19) cm

4¾ (5, 5¼, 5½, 5¾, 5¾)"
12 (12.5, 13.5, 14, 14.5, 14.5) cm

13¾ (15¼, 16½, 16½, 18, 18)"
35 (38.5, 42, 42, 45.5, 45.5) cm

Sleeve

13"
33 cm

11½ (13, 14½, 14½, 15¾, 15¾)"
29 (33, 37, 37, 40, 40) cm

DIVIDE FOR ARMHOLES

Next rnd: BO 5 (11, 15, 17, 19, 21) sts for left armhole, removing end-of-rnd m as you come to it, knit until there are 143 (149, 157, 167, 177, 187) front sts on needle after BO gap, BO 5 (11, 15, 17, 19, 21) sts for right armhole, knit to end—143 (149, 157, 167, 177, 187) sts each for front and back.

Place front sts on holder.

BACK
SHAPE ARMHOLES

Working back sts back and forth in rows in St st, purl WS 1 row. Cont in St st, dec 1 st at each end of needle every row 4 (4, 6, 8, 10, 12) times, then every RS row 6 (6, 5, 6, 7, 10) times, then every other RS row 4 (4, 4, 3, 2, 0) times—115 (121, 127, 133, 139, 143) sts rem. Work even in St st until 67 (73, 77, 83, 85, 87) armhole rows have been completed, ending with a WS row.

SHAPE NECK AND SHOULDERS

Next row: (RS) K40 (42, 44, 46, 48, 50), join new yarn, BO center 35 (37, 39, 41, 43, 43) sts, knit to end—40 (42, 44, 46, 48, 50) sts rem each side.

Working each side separately, at each neck edge BO 3 sts 3 times—31 (33, 35, 37, 39, 41) sts rem each side; 74 (80, 84, 90, 92, 94) armholes rows have been completed; armholes will measure about 7½ (8, 8½, 9, 9¼, 9½)" (19 [20.5, 21.5, 23, 23.5, 24] cm) after blocking. To cont neck shaping, at each neck edge BO 3 sts once, then BO 2 sts twice, then BO 1 st twice and *at the same time* for shoulder shaping, at each armhole edge BO 4 (4, 4, 5, 5, 5) sts 4 times, then BO 3 (4, 5, 4, 5, 6) sts 2 times—no sts rem.

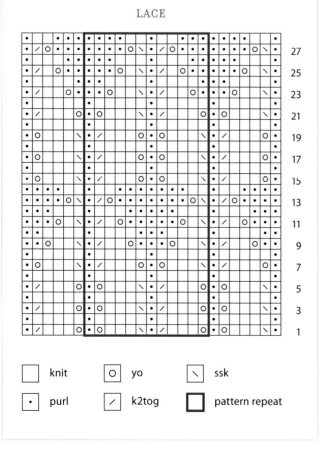

LACE

☐ knit	⊙ yo	╲ ssk
• purl	╱ k2tog	☐ pattern repeat

27
25
23
21
19
17
15
13
11
9
7
5
3
1

FRONT

Return 143 (149, 157, 167, 177, 187) held front sts to longer cir needle and rejoin yarns with WS facing. Working front sts back and forth in rows in St st, purl 1 WS row. Shape armholes as for back—115 (121, 127, 133, 139, 143) sts rem. Work even in St st until 33 (35, 39, 45, 47, 49) armhole rows have been completed, ending with a WS row.

SHAPE NECK AND SHOULDERS

Next row: (RS) K47 (50, 52, 54, 56, 58), join new yarn, BO center 21 (21, 23, 25, 27, 27) sts, knit to end—47 (50, 52, 54, 56, 58) sts rem each side. Working each side separately, at each neck edge BO 3 sts 3 times, then BO 2 sts 3 times—32 (35, 37, 39, 41, 43) sts rem each side. Dec 1 st at each neck edge every other row 5 times, then every 3 rows 3 times, then every 4 rows 2 (3, 3, 3, 3, 3) times—22 (24, 26, 28, 30, 32) sts rem each side. Work even in St st until 74 (80, 84, 90, 92, 94) armhole rows have been completed; armholes will measure about 7½ (8, 8½, 9, 9¼, 9½)" (19 [20.5, 21.5, 23, 23.5, 24] cm) after blocking. For shoulder shaping, at each armhole edge BO 4 (4, 4, 5, 5, 5) sts 4 times, then BO 3 (4, 5, 4, 5, 6) sts 2 times—no sts rem

Sleeves

With dpn, CO 98 (110, 122, 122, 134, 134) sts. Pm and join for working in rnds, being careful not to twist sts. If making longer sleeves, see Notes.

Rnd 1: *K1, pm, work Rnd 1 of Lace chart over 97 (109, 121, 121, 133, 133) sts.

Rnds 2–11: Working st before lace section in St st, work 10 rnds even, ending with Rnd 11 of chart.

Rnd 12: (inc rnd) M1 (see Glossary), k1, M1, sl m, work in lace patt to end—2 sts inc'd; 3 St sts at beg of rnd.

Rnds 13–25: Working new sts in St st, work 13 rnds even, ending with Rnd 25 of chart.

Rnd 26: (inc rnd) [K1f&b (see Glossary)] 2 times, k1, sl m, work in lace patt to end—2 sts inc'd; 5 St sts at beg of rnd.

Rnds 27 and 28: Working new sts in St st, work 2 rnds even, ending with Rnd 28 of chart.

Rnds 29–39: Working sts outside lace patt in St st, work Rnds 1–11 of chart.

Rnd 40: (Rnd 12 of chart) K1, [k1f&b] 2 times, k2, sl m, work in lace patt to end—2 sts inc'd; 7 St sts at beg of rnd.

Rnds 41–53: Working sts outside lace patt in St st, work Rnds 13–25 of chart.

Rnd 54: (Rnd 26 of chart): K2, [k1f&b] 2 times, k3, sl m, work in lace patt to end—2 sts inc'd; 9 St sts at beg of rnd.

Rnds 55 and 56: Working new sts in St st, work 2 rnds even, ending with Rnd 28 of chart.

Rnds 57–112: Cont in patts and changing to shorter cir needle when necessary, rep Rnds 1–28 of chart 2 more times and *at the same time* on Rnds 12 and 26 of each rep, inc 2 sts in St st section by knitting to 1 st before center St st, working [k1f&b] 2 times, then knitting rem St sts—114 (126, 138, 138, 150, 150) sts; 17 St sts at beg of rnd.

Rnds 113–140: Cont in patts, work Rnds 1–28 of chart even, ending last rnd 0 (0, 0, 0, 1, 2) st(s) before end-of-rnd m—piece will measure 13" (33 cm) after blocking.

SHAPE CAP

Next rnd: K6 (3, 1, 0, 0, 0), BO next 5 (11, 15, 17, 19, 21) sts, removing end-of-rnd m if necessary for your size, knit to end—109 (115, 123, 121, 131, 129) sts rem; BO will be centered over St st section.

Working St st back and forth in rows, purl 1 WS row. Cont in St st, dec 1 st at each end of needle

every row 4 (4, 4, 4, 4, 2) times, then every RS row 14 (16, 18, 23, 23, 25) times, then again every row 10 (8, 6, 0, 2, 0) times—53 (59, 67, 67, 73, 75) sts rem. BO 4 (4, 5, 5, 5, 5) sts at beg of next 4 rows—37 (43, 47, 47, 53, 55) sts rem. BO all sts.

fINISHING

NECKBAND

With yarn threaded on a tapestry needle, sew right shoulder seam. With longer cir needle and RS facing, pick up and knit 44 (50, 50, 50, 50, 50) sts along left front neck, 21 (21, 23, 25, 27, 27) sts across center front, 44 (50, 50, 50, 50, 50) sts along right front neck, 19 (20, 19, 19, 20, 20) sts along left back neck, 35 (37, 39, 41, 43, 43) sts across center back, and 20 (20, 20, 19, 20, 20) sts along left back neck—183 (198, 201, 204, 210, 210) sts total. Do not join. Work back and forth in rows as foll:

Row 1: (WS) *K1, yo, p2tog; rep from *.
Row 2: (RS) *K2, p1; rep from *.
BO all sts pwise on next WS row.

With yarn threaded on a tapestry needle, sew neckband and left shoulder seam. Weave in loose ends. Sew sleeves into armholes, easing to fit.

Wash in warm soapy water and gently roll in a towel to squeeze out excess water. Block to measurements, straightening pieces as necessary (see Notes), and leave to dry flat. Once dry, press carefully on the WS with a warm iron over a damp cloth.

MÄRTA
EMBROIDERED BAG

FINISHED SIZE

About 14¾" (37.5 cm) wide at base and 12" (30.5 cm) high, not including handles.

YARN

Sportweight (#2 Fine).
Shown here: Ullcentrum Öland 2-Thread Wool Yarn (100% wool; 328 yd [300 m]/100 g): petrol (teal; A), red (B), cream (C), 1 skein each; yellow (D), small amount.

NEEDLES

Size 3 mm (no exact U.S. equivalent; between U.S. size 2 and 3): 24" (60 cm) circular (cir). Adjust needle size if necessary to obtain the correct gauge.

NOTIONS

Tapestry needle; stitch holder (optional); ½ yd [0.5 m] of 36" (91.5 cm) or wider linen fabric for lining; sharp-point sewing needle and thread; one pair wooden purse handles with 10" to 11" (25.5 to 28 cm) wide slots.

GAUGE

27 stitches and 29½ rounds = 4" (10 cm) in charted color patterns, worked in rounds.

Inspired by the vibrant work of Märta Måås-Fjetterstöm, one of Sweden's foremost textile artists and pupil of Lilli Zickerman, who founded the Swedish Handicraft Association, the Märta bag is a lovely example of a well-designed, useful everyday object that is not only beautiful to look at but is beautiful to use.

Knitted in the round in Ullcentrum's fabulous 2-ply pure Swedish wool, the Märta bag is embroidered with simple cross-stitches, French knots, and duplicate-stitch details before being handwashed and slightly felted.

HEARTS AND FLOWERS

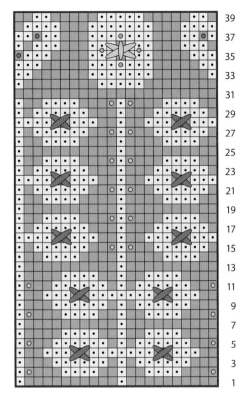
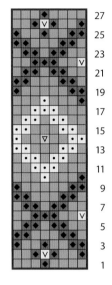

39
37
35
33
31
29
27
25
23
21
19
17
15
13
11
9
7
5
3
1

DIAMONDS

27
25
23
21
19
17
15
13
11
9
7
5
3
1

	A
	B
	C
V	knit with A, duplicate st with C
▽	knit with A, duplicate st with D
⊙	k with A, French knot with B
○	k with A, French knot with D
⊙	k with C, French knot with A
☐	pattern repeat
✕	small cross-stitch with B
	large cross-stitch and vertical straight stitch with D

BAG

With A, CO 200 sts. Place marker (pm) and join for working in rnds, being careful not to twist sts; rnd begins at side of bag where color changes between rnds will be less obvious. With A, knit 1 rnd. Work Rnds 1–27 of Diamonds chart. With A, knit 1 rnd.

Dec rnd: With A, *k1, ssk, k97; rep from * once more—198 sts rem.

Work Rnds 1–39 of Hearts and Flowers chart. With A, knit 5 rnds—piece measures 10" (25.5 cm) from CO. Place last 99 sts of rnd on holder (optional) for one side of bag or allow sts to rest on cable portion of cir needle while working the other side. Work the first 99 sts of rnd back and forth in rows with A as foll:

Row 1: (RS) K1, ssk, knit to last 3 sts, ssk, k1—2 sts dec'd.

Row 2: (WS) Purl.

Rep Rows 1 and 2 ten more times—77 sts rem; piece measures 13" (33 cm) from CO. BO these 77 sts. Return 99 held sts to cir needle if they are not already on the needle and rejoin A with RS facing. Rep Rows 1 and 2 a total of 11 times—77 sts rem. BO all sts.

FINISHING

Work embroidery (see Glossary for embroidery stitches) as indicated on charts as foll: With cream and yellow, work single duplicate stitches as shown on Diamonds chart. With red, work a small cross-stitch in the center of each small flower of Hearts and Flowers chart. In the middle of each large flower at the top of Hearts

and Flowers chart, work a large cross-stitch with a vertical straight stitch at its center using yellow. Work French knots with teal, red, and yellow as shown in Hearts and Flowers chart. Weave in loose ends.

Wash bag in warm soapy water, gently roll in a towel to squeeze out excess water, pull gently into shape, and allow to dry flat. When dry, press carefully with a warm iron over a damp cloth.

LINING

Using the knitted bag as a template, cut two pieces of linen lining fabric with a ½" (1.3 cm) seam allowance all the way around each piece. Sew lining pieces tog at the sides and across the bottom using sewing machine or sharp-point sewing needle, leaving the top 3" (7.5 cm) of each side unsewn. Press seams. Turn raw edges ½" (1.3 cm) to WS along upper part of lining and press. Turn lining WS out and place lining inside bag so wrong sides of bag and lining are touching. With sewing needle and thread, slip-stitch lining to bag along the shaped top selvedges and across the BO edges. Insert the BO edge of one side into the slot of one handle, fold upper edge of bag 1" (2.5 cm) to WS, and sew securely in place with sewing needle and thread. Rep for other handle.

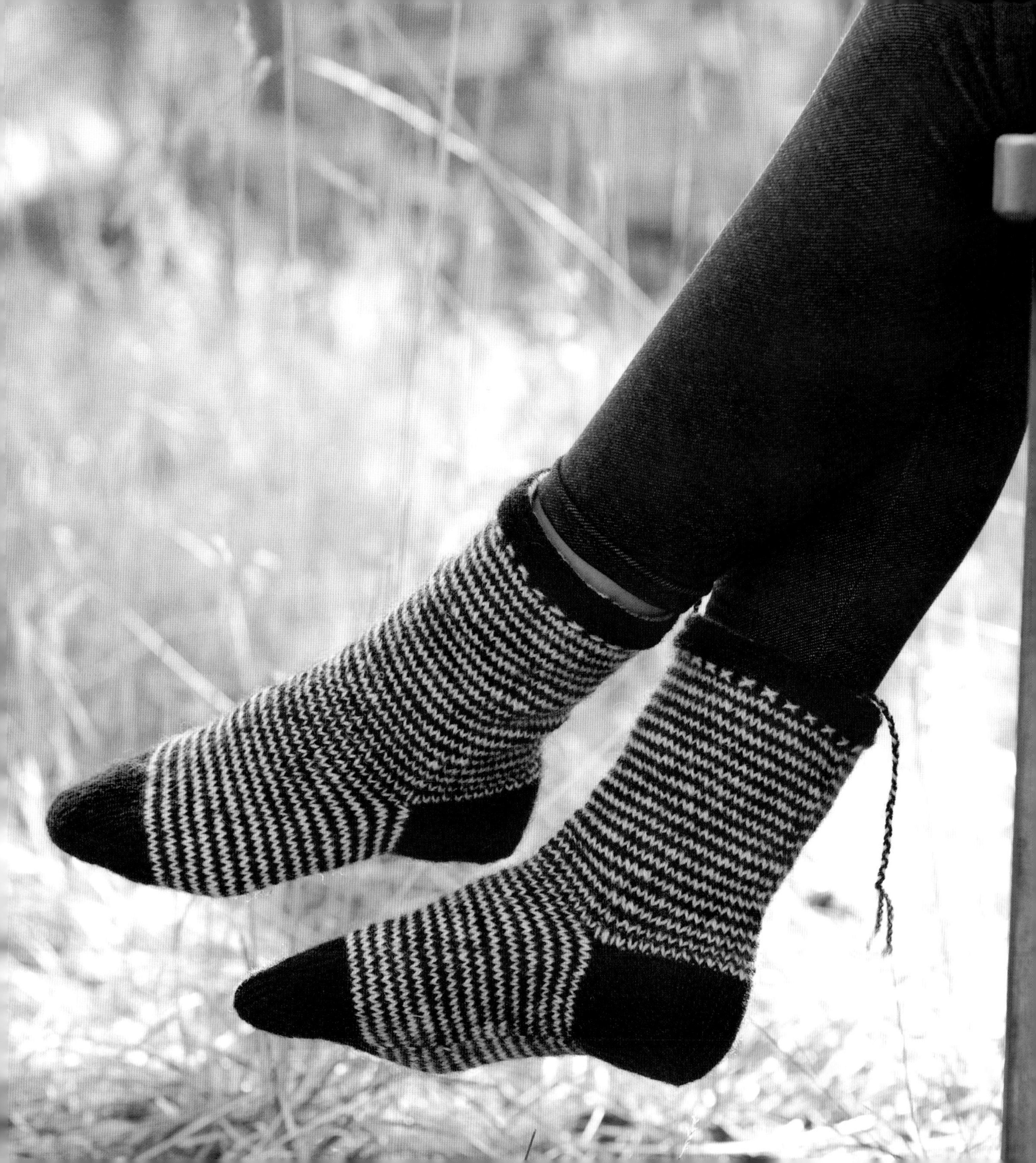

ULLA
TWINED SOCKS

FINISHED SIZE

About 8¼" (21 cm) foot circumference, 6¼"
(16 cm) leg length from CO to start of heel, and 9"
(23 cm) foot length from back of heel to tip of toe.
To fit women's U.S. shoe sizes 6–8, with instructions for making a longer foot.

YARN

Sportweight (#2 Fine).
Shown here: Ullcentrum Öland 2-Thread Wool Yarn
(100% wool; 328 yd [300 m]/100 g): red (A) and
cream (B), 1 skein each.

NEEDLES

Size 3 mm (no exact U.S. equivalent; between
U.S. sizes 2 and 3): set of 5 double-pointed (dpn).
Adjust needle size if necessary to obtain the
correct gauge.

NOTIONS

Marker (m); stitch holder; tapestry needle.

GAUGE

28 stitches and 28 rounds = 4" (10 cm) in twined
stockinette, worked in rounds.

There are many fine examples of handsomely
patterned twined knitted socks in the Nordiska
Museet in Stockholm. These socks were usually
knitted in one or two colors—often white, red, or
naturals—and included patterned crook-stitch or
chain-loop borders. These patterned borders were
not only decorative but functional as the "drawing
in" nature of the crook stitches proved useful for
keeping the socks up.

These socks are knitted with Ullcentrum's
2-thread pure wool on five needles, with twined purl
stitch and simple embroidery details, and, of course,
a twined tassel.

NOTES

· In order to have two working strands of each color, wind each skein into two balls.

· When decreasing in twined knitting, work k2tog or k2tog through back loops (tbl) in the ordinary manner, using the correct strand to maintain the alternation of the twined strands.

· The strands will twist around each other as you work. To undo the twist, periodically allow the sock to dangle and twirl freely in midair.

Stitch Guide

TWINED KNITTING

*With both strands in back, insert right needle into next st on left needle as if to knit, bring the strand farthest from the tip of the right needle *over* the other strand, and use it to knit the stitch; rep from * alternating the 2 strands and bringing each strand over the one used before.

TWINED PURLING

*With both strands in front, insert right needle into next st on left needle as if to purl, bring the strand farthest from the tip of the right needle *under* the other strand, and use it to purl the stitch; rep from * alternating the 2 strands and bringing each strand under the one used before.

Edging

Using the twined method (see page 138), CO 74 sts. Arrange sts on 4 dpn so that there are 19 sts on Needle 1, 18 sts on Needle 2, 19 sts on Needle 3, and 18 sts on Needle 4. Place marker (pm) and join for working in rnds, being careful not to twist sts; rnd begins at center back leg. Work edging with 2 strands of A as foll:

Rnds 1 and 2: Work 2 rnds twined purling (see Stitch Guide).

Rnds 3 and 4: Work 2 rnds twined knitting (see Stitch Guide).

Rnds 5–8: Rep Rnds 1–4.

Rnd 9: Work 1 rnd twined knitting—piece measures about 1" (2.5 cm) from CO.

Leg

Join 2 strands of B. Work twined knitting in stripes as foll:

Rnd 1: With B, knit.

Rnd 2: With A, knit.

Rnd 3: With B, knit.

Rnd 4: (dec rnd) With A, *k1, ssk (see Notes), work to end of needle; rep from * 3 more times—1 st dec'd each needle; 70 sts total.

Rnds 5, 7, 9, and 11: With B, knit.

Rnds 6, 8, 10, and 12: With A, knit

Rnds 13–16: Rep Rnds 1–4—66 sts.

Rnds 17–24: Rep Rnds 5 and 6 four times.

Rnds 25–32: Rep Rnds 1–4 two times—58 sts; 15 sts each on Needle 1 and Needle 3; 14 sts each on Needle 2 and Needle 4.

Rnds 33–36: Rep Rnds 5 and 6 two times—leg measures 6¼" (16 cm) from CO. Break off B.

TWINED CAST-ON

Leaving long tails for braiding later, make a slip-knot with 2 strands of A and 1 strand of B held tog, and place the slipknot on the right needle; the slipknot does not count as a CO st. Hold B in your left hand and the 2 strands of A in your right hand **(Figure 1)**. Loop B around the left thumb and insert right needle tip into the loop as if to start a long-tail cast-on, wrap one strand of A around the needle as if to knit **(Figure 2)**, draw up a stitch onto the right needle, drop the B loop from the left thumb **(Figure 3)**, and tighten the new st. *Loop B around left thumb again, insert right needle tip into the loop, bring the strand of A farthest from the right needle tip over the previous strand of A used, wrap it around the right needle as if to knit, draw up a stitch, drop B loop from left thumb, and tighten; rep from * until the required number of sts are CO, alternating strands of A and bringing each strand over the one used before. Break off B. Drop the slipknot from the needle before joining in the rnd, but do not untie it yet.

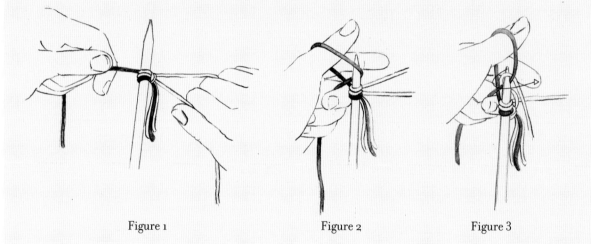

Figure 1   Figure 2   Figure 3

HEEL

Cont in twined knitting with A, k15 to end of Needle 1, place 29 sts from Needle 2 and Needle 3 on a holder to work later for instep, use the backward-loop method (see Glossary) alternating strands to CO 29 sts across sole side of heel, k14 to end of Needle 4—58 sts. Arrange sts so that there are 14 sts on Needle 1, 15 sts on Needle 2, 14 sts on Needle 3, and 15 sts on Needle 4. Cont in twined knitting, knit 2 rnds.

SHAPE HEEL

Cont in twined knitting as foll:

Rnd 1: On Needle 1, knit to last 3 sts, k2tog, k1; on Needle 2, k1, k2tog through back loops (tbl), knit to end; on Needle 3, knit to last 3 sts, k2tog, k1; on Needle 4, k1, k2tog tbl, knit to end—4 sts dec'd.

Rnd 2: Knit.

Rep Rnds 1 and 2 once more—50 sts rem. Rep Rnd 1 (dec every rnd) 10 times—10 sts rem; 2 sts each on Needle 1 and Needle 3; 3 sts each on Needle 2 and Needle 4. Break yarn, leaving a 12" (30.5 cm) tail for grafting. Place sts from Needles 1 and 2 on the same dpn, then place sts of Needles 3 and 4 on the same dpn—5 sts each on 2 needles. Use the Kitchener st (see Glossary) to graft sts tog—heel measures about 2½" (6.5 cm) from sts CO at sole side of heel.

FOOT

Hold sock with heel pointing down and RS of sole side of heel facing. Rejoin 2 strands of B to center of CO heel sts. With alternating strands of B and Needle 1, pick up and knit 14 sts from center of CO to side of foot; with Needle 2, work twined knitting across first 15 held instep sts; with Needle 3, work twined knitting across rem 14 held instep sts; with Needle 4 and alternating strands, pick up and knit 15 sts from side of foot to center of CO—58 sts; 14 sts each on Needle 1 and Needle 3; 15 sts each on Needle 2 and Needle 4; rnd begins at center of sole. Rejoin A, and work 26 rnds in twined knitting, beg with A, alternating 1 rnd each of A and B, and ending with a rnd of B—foot measures about 4" (10 cm) from pick-up rnd, and 6½" (16.5 cm) from end

of heel. Break off B. *Note:* For a foot longer than the 9" (23 cm) socks shown, work additional rnds of A and B until foot measures 2½" (6.5 cm) less than desired length, ending with a rnd of B.

TOE

Cont in twined knitting with A, knit 2 rnds. Rep Rnds 1 and 2 of heel shaping 2 times, then rep Rnd 1 of heel shaping (dec every rnd) 10 times—10 sts rem; 2 sts each on Needle 1 and Needle 3; 3 sts each on Needle 2 and Needle 4. Break yarn, leaving a 12" (30.5 cm) tail. Thread the tail through rem sts, pull tight to close the hole, and fasten off on the WS.

FINISHING

Undo the CO slipknot and work a 3-strand braid using the CO tails. Tie the end of the braid in an overhand knot and trim the ends even. Weave in loose ends.

With B threaded on a tapestry needle, embroider a line of cross-stitches (see Glossary) along Rnds 7 and 8 of the top edging, working each cross-stitch 2 knit sts wide and 2 knit sts high, with 1 knit st between each pair of cross-stitches and 2 knit sts between the cross-stitches on each side of the center back leg as shown.

Wash in warm soapy water, gently roll in a towel to squeeze out excess water, pull gently into shape, and leave flat to dry. Once dry, press carefully with a warm iron over a damp cloth.

OTTILIA
TWINED MITTENS

FINISHED SIZE

About 8" (20.5 cm) hand circumference. To fit a woman's medium to large hand.

YARN

Sportweight (#2 Fine).
Shown here: Ullcentrum Öland 2-Thread Wool Yarn (100% wool; 328 yd [300 m]/100 g): cream (A), 1 skein; yellow (B) and medium gray (C), small amount of each.

NEEDLES

Size 3 mm (no exact U.S. equivalent; between U.S. size 2 and 3): set of 5 double-pointed (dpn). Adjust needle size if necessary to obtain the correct gauge.

NOTIONS

Marker (m); waste yarn for stitch holder; tapestry needle.

GAUGE

30 stitches and 30 rounds = 4" (10 cm) in twined stockinette stitch, worked in rounds.

I have long admired the outfits that the trolls and gnomes wear in John Bauer's illustrations of Swedish folk and fairy tales. I especially like their tasseled and embroidered mittens. As trolls spend a lot of their time in woods and mountains, they would need extra warm and sturdy knitwear. So, they surely would have used the twined method of knitting.

These wonderfully warm Ottilia mittens are knitted with Ullcentrum's 2-strand pure wool, which is ideally suited to twined knitting. They have twined purl and chain-path stitch details and, once finished and embroidered, they are slightly felted.

NOTES

· In order to have two working strands of colors A and B, wind each skein into two balls.

· The strands will twist around each other as you work. To undo the twist, periodically allow the mitten to dangle and twirl freely in midair.

· When decreasing in twined knitting, work k2tog or k2tog through back loops (tbl) in the ordinary manner, using the correct strand to maintain the alternation of the twined strands.

· With working k1f&b increases (see Glossary) in twined knitting, alternate the strands in the correct order when working the 2 stitches.

STITCH GUIDE

TWINED KNITTING

*With both strands in back, insert right needle into next st on left needle as if to knit, bring the strand farthest from the tip of the right needle *over* the other strand, and use it to knit the stitch; rep from * alternating the 2 strands and bringing each strand over the one used before.

TWINED PURLING

*With both strands in front, insert right needle into next st on left needle as if to purl, bring the strand farthest from the tip of the right needle *under* the other strand, and use it to purl the stitch; rep from * alternating the 2 strands and bringing each strand under the one used before.

CROOK STITCH
(ODD NUMBER OF STS)

Join 2 strands of B; either strand can be chosen as the front strand for the first stitch of Rnd 1.

Rnd 1: With B, bring strand farthest from right needle tip to front where it will rem throughout. P1 with front strand, *k1 with back strand, p1 with front strand; rep from *.

Bring front strand of B to back.

Rnd 2: With A, k1 with strand farthest from right needle tip. Bring strand that is now farthest from right needle tip to front where it will rem throughout. *P1 with front strand, k1 with back strand; rep from *. Bring front strand of A to back.

Rnd 3: With B, rep Rnd 1.

Bring both strands of B to back and cut off B.

MITTEN EMBROIDERY

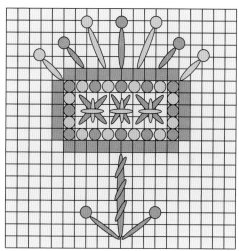

 Duplicate st with C

Stem stitch
in appropriate color

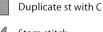 Cross-stitch
in appropriate color

French knot
in appropriate color

Left Mitten

Using the twined with double bead method (see page 116), CO 61 sts. Arrange sts so there are 15 sts each on Needles 1, 2, and 3 and 16 sts on Needle 4. Place marker (pm) and join for working in rnds, being careful not to twist sts; rnd begins at little finger side of hand. With A, work 1 rnd of twined purling (see Stitch Guide). With A, work 14 rnds twined knitting (see Stitch Guide)—piece measures 2" (5 cm) from CO. Work Rnds 1–3 of crook stitch (see Stitch Guide). Cont in twined knitting with A, knit 2 rnds.

Next rnd: Knit to last 3 sts of Needle 4, k2tog (see Notes), k1—60 sts rem; 15 sts on each needle; piece measures 2¾" (7 cm) from CO.

SHAPE GUSSET

Inc rnd: On Needle 1, knit; on Needle 2, knit to last 2 sts k1f&b (see Notes), k1; on Needles 3 and 4, knit—1 st inc'd at end of Needle 2.

Rep the inc rnd 9 more times—70 sts; 25 sts on Needle 2; 15 sts each on the other 3 needles. Knit 8 rnds.

Next rnd: On Needle 1, knit; on Needle 2, k7, place next 18 sts on holder, use the backward-loop method (see Glossary) to CO 8 sts; on Needles 3 and 4, knit—60 sts; 15 sts each needle.

UPPER HAND

Cont even in twined knitting until piece measures 8" (20.5 cm) from CO, or to the tip of the little finger.

SHAPE TOP

Dec rnd: *On Needle 1, k1, k2tog through back loops (tbl; see Glossary), knit to end; on Needle 2, knit to last 3 sts, k2tog, k1; rep from * for Needles 3 and 4—4 sts dec'd; 1 st from each needle. Rep the dec rnd 12 more times—8 sts rem; piece measures 9¾" (25 cm) from CO. Cut yarn, leaving a 10" (25.5 cm) tail. Thread tail on a tapestry needle, draw through rem sts, pull tight to close hole, and fasten off on WS.

THUMB

Return 18 held thumb sts to dpn and join 2 strands of A with RS facing. Working in twined knitting, k18 thumb sts, then pick up and knit 8 sts from base of sts CO over thumb gap for hand—26 sts total. Arrange sts so there are 7 sts each on Needles 1 and 3, and 6 sts each in Needles 2 and 4; rnd begins at start of palm side of thumb. Cont even in twined knitting until thumb measures 1¾" (4.5 cm), or to middle of thumbnail.

Dec rnd: *On Needle 1, knit to last 3 sts, k2tog, k1; on Needle 2, k1, k2tog tbl, knit to end; rep from * for Needles 3 and 4—4 sts dec'd; 1 st from each needle.

Rep the dec rnd 3 more times—10 sts rem. Cut yarn, leaving a 10" (25.5 cm) tail. Thread tail on a tapestry needle, draw through rem sts, pull tight to close hole, and fasten off on WS.

RIGHT MITTEN

CO and work as for left mitten to start of gusset shaping—60 sts rem; 15 sts on each needle; piece measures 2¾" (7 cm) from CO.

SHAPE GUSSET

Inc rnd: On Needles 1 and 2, knit; on Needle 3, k1, k1f&b, knit to end; on Needle 4, knit—1 st inc'd at beg of Needle 3.

Rep the inc rnd 9 more times—70 sts; 25 sts on Needle 3; 15 sts each on the other 3 needles. Knit 8 rnds.

Next rnd: On Needles 1 and 2, knit; on Needle 3, place first 18 sts on holder, use the backward-loop method to CO 8 sts, k7; on Needle 4, knit—60 sts; 15 sts each needle.

UPPER HAND AND SHAPE TOP

Work as for left mitten.

THUMB

Return 18 held thumb sts to dpn and join 2 strands of A with RS facing. Working in twined knitting, k18 thumb sts, then pick up and knit 8 sts from base of sts CO over thumb gap for hand—26 sts total. Knit the first 6 sts again—these sts will become Needle 4. Arrange rem sts so there are 7 sts each on Needles 1 and 3 and 6 sts on Needle 2; rnd begins on palm side of hand with sts of Needle 1. Cont even in twined knitting until thumb measures 1¾" (4.5 cm), or to middle of thumbnail. Work dec rnds and finish as for left thumb.

FINISHING

Undo the CO slipknot and work the tails in a 3-strand braid. Tie the end of the braid in an overhand knot and trim the ends even. Weave in loose ends.

Work embroidery (see Glossary for embroidery stitches) as foll: With C, work duplicate-stitch rectangle centered on back of hand, with bottom of rectangle about 1½" (3.8 cm) above last rnd of crook stitch. With C, work 3 large cross-stitches inside rectangle, then work a small cross-stitch with B in the center of each large cross-stitch as shown. With B and C, work French knots inside rectangle. With B and C, work short radiating lines of stem stitches ending in French knots above the rectangle as shown. With C, work a vertical straight stitch below the rectangle, then couch this stitch with short diagonal straight stitches as shown. Work 2 straight stitches ending in French knots to form a V at the bottom of the vertical line.

Wash mittens in hot soapy water (the mittens have a better finish and fit if slightly felted), gently roll in a towel to squeeze out excess water, pull gently into shape, and leave to dry flat. Once dry, press carefully with a warm iron over a damp cloth.

GLOSSARY

ABBREVIATIONS

beg(s) begin(s); beginning

BO bind off

CC contrasting color

cm centimeter(s)

cn cable needle

CO cast on

cont continue(s); continuing

dec(s) decrease(s); decreasing

dpn double-pointed needles

foll follow(s); following

g gram(s)

inc(s) increase(s); increasing

k knit

k1f&b knit into the front and back of same stitch

kwise knitwise, as if to knit

m marker(s)

MC main color

mm millimeter(s)

M1 make one (increase)

p purl

p1f&b purl into front and back of same stitch

patt(s) pattern(s)

psso pass slipped stitch over

pwise purlwise, as if to purl

rem remain(s); remaining

rep repeat(s); repeating

rev St st reverse stockinette stitch

rnd(s) round(s)

RS right side

sl slip

sl st slip st (slip 1 stitch purlwise unless otherwise indicated)

ssk slip 2 stitches knitwise, one at a time, from the left needle to right needle, insert left needle tip through both front loops and knit together from this position (1 stitch decrease)

st(s) stitch(es)

St st stockinette stitch

tbl through back loop

tog together

WS wrong side

wyb with yarn in back

wyf with yarn in front

yd yard(s)

yo yarnover

* repeat starting point

** repeat all instructions between asterisks

( ) alternate measurements and/or instructions

[ ] work instructions as a group a specified number of times

BIND-OFF

THREE-NEEDLE BIND-OFF

Place the stitches to be joined onto two separate needles and hold the needles parallel so that the right sides of knitting face together. Insert a third needle into the first stitch on each of two needles **(Figure 1)** and knit them together as one stitch **(Figure 2)**, *knit the next stitch on each needle the same way, then use the left needle tip to lift the first stitch over the second and off the needle **(Figure 3)**. Repeat from * until no stitches remain on first two needles. Cut yarn and pull tail through last stitch to secure.

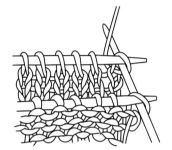

Figure 1

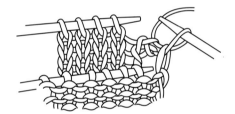

Figure 2

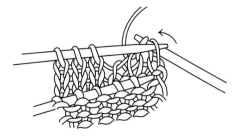

Figure 3

CAST-ONS

BACKWARD-LOOP CAST-ON

*Loop working yarn and place it on needle backward so that it doesn't unwind. Repeat from *.

CABLE CAST-ON

If there are no stitches on the needle, make a slipknot of working yarn and place it on the needle, then use the knitted method to cast-on one more stitch—two stitches on needle. Hold needle with working yarn in your left hand with the wrong side of the work facing you. *Insert right needle *between* the first two stitches on left needle **(Figure 1)**, wrap yarn around needle as if to knit, draw yarn through **(Figure 2)**, and place new loop on left needle **(Figure 3)** to form a new stitch. Repeat from * for the desired number of stitches, always working between the first two stitches on the left needle.

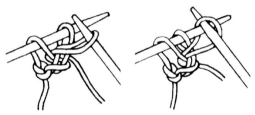

Figure 1

Figure 2   Figure 3

KNITTED CAST-ON

Make a slipknot of working yarn and place it on the left needle if there are no stitches already there. *Use the right needle to knit the first stitch (or slipknot) on left needle **(Figure 1)** and place new loop onto left needle to form a new stitch **(Figure 2)**. Repeat from * for the desired number of stitches, always working into the last stitch made.

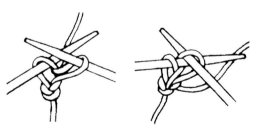

Figure 1   Figure 2

CROCHET

SLIP-STITCH CROCHET: SL ST CR
*Insert hook into stitch, yarn over hook and draw a loop through both the stitch and the loop already on hook. Repeat from * for the desired number of stitches.

CROCHET CHAIN: CH
Make a slipknot and place it on crochet hook if there isn't a loop already on the hook. *Yarn over hook and draw through loop on hook. Repeat from * for the desired number of stitches. To fasten off, cut yarn and draw end through last loop formed.

DECREASES

KNIT 2 TOGETHER THROUGH BACK LOOPS: K2TOGTBL
Knit two stitches together through the loops on the back of the needle.

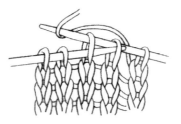

SLIP, SLIP, KNIT: SSK
Slip two stitches individually knitwise (**Figure 1**), insert left needle tip into the front of these two slipped stitches, then use the right needle to knit them together through their back loops (**Figure 2**).

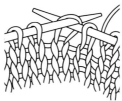
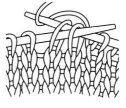

Figure 1   Figure 2

SLIP, SLIP, PURL: SSP

Holding yarn in front, slip two stitches individually knitwise **(Figure 1)**, then slip these two stitches back onto left needle (they will be twisted on the needle) and purl them together through their back loops **(Figure 2)**.

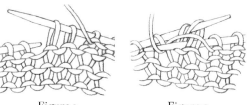

Figure 1   Figure 2

EMBROIDERY

CROSS-STITCH

Bring threaded needle out from back to front at lower left edge of the knitted stitch (or stitches) to be covered. Working from left to right, *insert needle at the upper right edges of the same stitch(es) and bring it back out at the lower left edge of the adjacent stitch, directly below and in line with the insertion point. Work from right to left to work the other half of the cross.

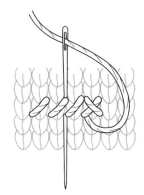

DUPLICATE STITCH

Bring threaded needle out from back to front at the base of the V of the knitted stitch you want to cover. *Working right to left, pass needle in and out under the stitch in the row above it and back into the base of the same stitch. Bring needle back out at the base of the V of the next stitch to the left. Repeat from * for desired number of stitches.

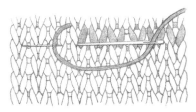

FRENCH KNOT

Bring threaded needle out of knitted background from back to front, wrap yarn around needle three times, and use your thumb to hold the wraps in place while you insert the needle into the background a short distance from where it came out. Pull the needle through the wraps into the background.

STEM STITCH

Bring threaded needle out of knitted background from back to front at the center of a knitted stitch. *Insert the needle into the upper right edge of the next stitch to the right, then out again at the center of the stitch below. Repeat from * as desired.

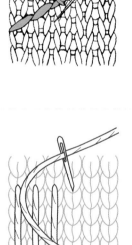

STRAIGHT STITCH

Bring threaded needle in and out of background to form a dashed line.

GRAFTING

KITCHENER STITCH

Arrange stitches on two needles so that there is the same number of stitches on each needle. Hold the needles parallel to each other with wrong sides of the knitting together. Allowing about ½" (1.3 cm) per stitch to be grafted, thread matching yarn on a tapestry needle. Work from right to left as follows:

Step 1 Bring tapestry needle through the first stitch on the front needle as if to purl and leave the stitch on the needle (**Figure 1**).

Step 2 Bring tapestry needle through the first stitch on the back needle as if to knit and leave that stitch on the needle (**Figure 2**).

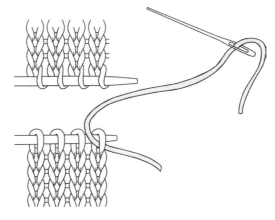

Figure 1

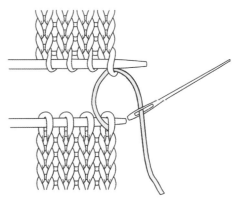

Figure 2

Step 3 Bring tapestry needle through the first front stitch as if to knit and slip this stitch off the needle, then bring tapestry needle through the next front stitch as if to purl and leave this stitch on the needle **(Figure 3)**.

Step 4 Bring tapestry needle through the first back stitch as if to purl and slip this stitch off the needle, then bring tapestry needle through the next back stitch as if to knit and leave this stitch on the needle **(Figure 4)**.

Repeat Steps 3 and 4 until one stitch remains on each needle, adjusting the tension to match the rest of the knitting as you go. To finish, bring tapestry needle through the front stitch as if to knit and slip this stitch off the needle, then bring tapestry needle through the back stitch as if to purl and slip this stitch off the needle.

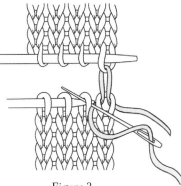

Figure 3

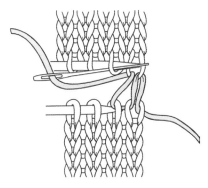

Figure 4

INCREASES

BAR INCREASE: K1 F&B

Knit into a stitch but leave it on the left needle **(Figure 1)**, then knit through the back loop of the same stitch **(Figure 2)** and slip the original stitch off the needle **(Figure 3)**.

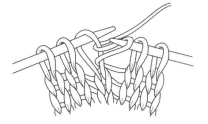
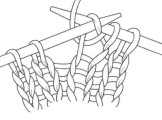
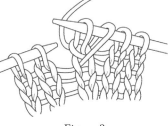

Figure 1   Figure 2   Figure 3

RAISED MAKE-ONE

Note: Use the left slant if no direction of slant is specified.

LEFT SLANT (M1L)

With left needle tip, lift the strand between the last knitted stitch and the first stitch on the left needle from front to back **(Figure 1)**, then knit the lifted loop through the back **(Figure 2)**.

Figure 1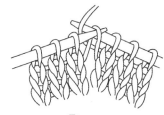

Figure 2

NORTHERN knits

RIGHT SLANT (M1R)

With left needle tip, lift the strand between the needles from back to front **(Figure 1)**. Knit the lifted loop through the front **(Figure 2)**.

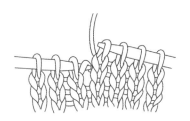

Figure 1

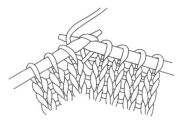

Figure 2

PURLWISE (M1P)

With left needle tip, lift he strand between the needles from back to front **(Figure 1)**, then purl the lifted loop through the front **(Figure 2)**.

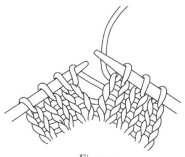

Figure 1

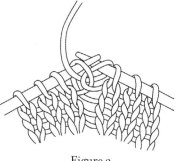

Figure 2

Seams

MATTRESS STITCH

Place the pieces to be seamed on a table, right sides facing up. Begin at the lower edge and work upward as follows for your stitch pattern:

STOCKINETTE STITCH WITH 1-STITCH SEAM ALLOWANCE

Insert threaded needle under one bar between the two edge stitches on one piece, then under the corresponding bar plus the bar above it on the other piece (**Figure 1**). *Pick up the next two bars on the first piece (**Figure 2**), then the next two bars on the other (**Figure 3**). Repeat from *, ending by picking up the last bar or pair of bars on the first piece.

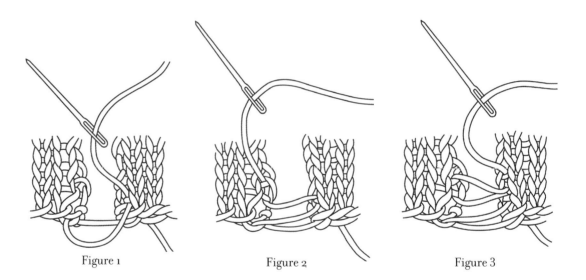

Figure 1   Figure 2   Figure 3

STOCKINETTE STITCH WITH ½-STITCH SEAM ALLOWANCE

To reduce bulk in the mattress-stitch seam, work as for the 1-stitch seam allowance but pick up the bars in the center of the edge stitches instead of between the last two stitches.

WHIPSTITCH SEAM

Hold pieces to be sewn together so that the edges to be seamed are even with each other. With yarn threaded on a tapestry needle, *insert needle through both layers from back to front, then bring needle to back. Repeat from *, keeping even tension on the seaming yarn.

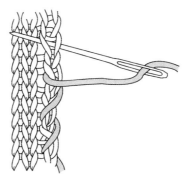

TASSEL

Cut a piece of cardboard 4" (10 cm) wide by the desired length of the tassel plus 1" (2.5 cm). Wrap yarn to desired thickness around cardboard. Cut a short length of yarn and tie tightly around one end of wrapped yarn **(Figure 1)**. Cut yarn loops at other end. Cut another piece of yarn and wrap tightly around loops a short distance below top knot to form tassel neck. Knot securely, thread ends onto tapestry needle, and pull to center of tassel **(Figure 2)**. Trim ends.

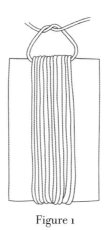

Figure 1

Figure 2

SOURCES FOR SUPPLIES

Alafoss
Ístex
PO Box 140
270 Mosfellsbær
ICELAND
www.istex.is

Jamieson & Smith
90 North Rd.,
Lerwick,
Shetland Isles
ZE1 OPQ
www.shetlandwool.org

Dale of Norway
4750 Shelburne Rd.
Ste. 20
Shelburne, VT 05482
www.dale.no

Loðband
Ístex
PO Box 140
270 Mosfellsbær
ICELAND
www.istex.is

Ístex
PO Box 140
270 Mosfellsbær
ICELAND
www.istex.is

Ullcentrum Öland
Byrumvägen 59
SE-380 74 Löttorp
Sweden
www.ullcentrum.com

INDEX

backward-loop cast-on 148
bar increase (k1f&b) 154
bind-off 147
Bohus Stickning 111

cable cast-on 148
cast-ons 148
Cracaus, Magna Brita 110
crochet chain (ch) 149
crochet stitches 149
cross-stitch 150

Dale of Norway 77
Dale, Unn Søiland 77
decreases 149–150
duplicate stitch 150

embroidery stitches 150–151
Emstad, Marit 76

Fair Isle 44–45
fisherman sweaters 76, 110
French knot 151

grafting 152–153
Handarbetets Vänner 111

Iceland 10–11
increases 154–155

lice stitch 76, 79

Jacobsson, Emma 111

Kitchener stitch 152–153
knitted cast-on 148
knit 2 together through back loops
   (k2togtbl) 149

Larsson, Karin and Carl 111
lopi yarn 11

make-one, raised 154–155

Nordiska Museet 111, 135
Norway 76–77
seams 156–157
shawls 45
Shetland 44–45
Skansen Museum 111
slip, slip, knit (ssk) 149
slip, slip, purl (ssp) 150
slip-stitch crochet (sl st cr) 149

stem stitch 151
stitches, crochet chain (ch) 149;
   cross-stitch 150; duplicate 150;
   French knot 151; Kitchener 152–153;
   knit 2 together through back loops
   (k2togtbl) 149; make-one, raised
   increase 154–155; mattress 156; slip,
   slip, knit (ssk) 149; slip, slip, purl
   (ssp) 150; slip-stitch crochet (sl st)
   149; stem 151; straight 151;
   whipstitch 157
straight stitch 151
sweater, fisherman 76, 110
Sweden 110–111
Swedish Handicraft Association 111

tassel 157
three-needle bind-off 147
twined cast-on 138
twined cast-on with double bead 116
twined knitting 110
two-ended knitting 110

Zickerman, Lilli 111

CREATE EVEN MORE TRADITION-INSPIRED KNITWEAR
WITH THESE RESOURCES FROM INTERWEAVE

Inca Knits
Designs Inspired by
South American Folk Tradition
Marianne Isager Collection
ISBN 978-1-59668-116-3
$24.95

New England Knits
Timeless Knitwear
with a Modern Twist
*Cecily Glowik MacDonald
and Melissa LaBarre*
ISBN 978-1-59668-180-4
$24.95

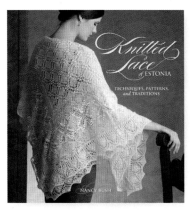

Knitted Lace of Estonia
Techniques, Patterns,
and Traditions
Nancy Bush
ISBN 978-1-59668-053-1
$24.95